Who's Afraid Of The Big Bad Wolf? — A Handbook On How To Defeat The 1%

Who's Afraid Of The Big Bad Wolf? — A Handbook On How To Defeat The 1%

Gabriel of Urantia

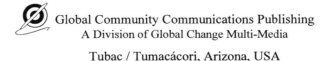
Global Community Communications Publishing
A Division of Global Change Multi-Media

Tubac / Tumacácori, Arizona, USA

© 2012 Global Community Communications Alliance

All rights reserved. No part of this book shall be reproduced, translated, or transmitted in any form or by any means, electronic, mechanical, magnetic, photographic including photocopying, recording, or by any information storage and retrieval system, without prior written permission of Global Community Communications Publishing. No patent liability is assumed with respect to the use of the information contained herein. Although every precaution has been taken in the preparation of this book, the publisher and author assume no responsibility for errors or omissions. Neither is any liability assumed for damages resulting from the use of the information contained herein.

ISBN 978-1-937919-03-0

Global Community Communications Publishing
P.O. Box 1613, Tubac, Arizona 85646 USA
(520) 603-9932

e-mail: info@gccpublishing.org
gccpublishing.org

Cover Design — Cooperation in action:
Fusion idea of Occupy Movement with Spiritualution[SM] Movement
— Gabriel of Urantia
Original pencil drawing of arms — Keea
Idea of tattoos on arms — Gabriel of Urantia
Graphics of the front cover — Amadon DellErba

My gratitude to Ionia Redman
for all her work in book layout & design. Ionia has a
Bachelor of Science from Michigan State University.

My appreciation to LaTaYea Calviero,
my private secretary, typist, and grammar coach, who has a
Bachelor of Arts from Pennsylvania State University.

CONTENTS

PREFACE............................. ix

INTRODUCTION TO THE BOOK............ 1

LET'S OCCUPY
by Niánn Emerson Chase 3

ARTICLES BY GABRIEL OF URANTIA:

Defining The Spiritualution^{SM} Movement—
A Spiritual Revolution—In Reference To
The 99% Movement And Occupy Wall Street.
What The People Must Do To Win Over
The Power Elite........................... 9

The Cry Of The Indigenous Is The Cry Of All
Of Us In The 99%. What Is The Baby Boomers'
And The X Generation's Responsibility?....... 16

Pseudo-Activism And University Students.
The Great American Dream Is Over, But Many
Millions Of Americans Still Hang On To False
Hopes. The 99% Are Beginning To Awaken
To The Entrapment Of The False Powers.
Is There An Answer To The Future? 24

The Occupy Movement In Relationship To
George Washington, The Colonists,
And How They Won The Revolution 32

The Occupiers Must Learn How To Use
The Creator To Win Over The Power-Elite
And Their Soldiers Of Gas-Destruction 40

The Higher-Consciousness-Handicapped
Presidential Nominees, Our Current
Compromising-Consciousness President,
And The Need For Both To Lean On
Somebody Or Fall......................... 49

The Judicial System: Why It Does Not Work
And How It Can. Occupy The Courts.......... 56

*A Series Of 3 Articles On Community Building
And Survival In Times Of Economic Crisis*

    PART 1 — Community Living—The
    Answer As To How To Defeat The 1%.
    The Establishment Of Subcultures.......... 62

    PART 2 — Substitutes For Community
    Living. Modern Society And The Breakdown
    Of Having All Things In Common,
    Including Interpersonal Relationships 72

    PART 3 — The Loneliness, Stress, Isolation,
    And Lack Of Human Compassion And
    Support Of Brothers And Sisters Existing
    In Urban Life. The Need For Community
    And Coming Back To Nature 81

A Series Of 3 Articles In Relationship To The Deterioration Of The Earth And All Its Systems —Climatic, Resources, Food, Economic, And Consciousness

> PART 1 — The Occupy Movement Needs To Fuse With The Spiritualution℠ Movement To Win Against The 1% 89
>
> PART 2 — The Invisible War 99
>
> PART 3 — The "Occupy Movement" Is Actually The Right Name Because The "99%" Is A Misnomer. The Leftover Middle Class Are The Silent Apathy-ites. . . . 112
>
> True Leaders—Where Can You Find Them? How Can You Identify The False Leaders? Why Do We Need Leaders? 121
>
> To Achieve Cultural And Religious Unity In A One-World Government Outside Of The Control Of The 1%, A Global Spiritualution Is The Only Answer 134–149
>
> Global Interdependence Day 150

ARTICLES BY OTHER AUTHORS:

How Do You Choose To Occupy This World? by Niánn Emerson Chase 151

The Occupy Movement Needs Leadership Now by BenDameean Steinhardt. 160

Occupation Of The Nation
by Kazarian Giannangelo 165

Submission And Transparency
Versus Rebellion And Darkness.
Inside Anarchy And The Black Bloc
by Amadon DellErba 175

PHOTO GALLERY 190

THE SPIRITUALUTION℠ MOVEMENT 239

INFORMATION ON RECENT
AND PENDING LEGISLATION AND
COMMENTS ON GUN CONTROL 242

GLOBAL CHANGE MUSIC℠ 244

BE AWARE PROCLAMATION
& ANSWERS 245

UNOCCUPY YOUR COUCH — 10 POINTS
TO BECOME PROACTIVE IN 253

5 PRINCIPLES OF PLANETARY PEACE ... 255

SONG LYRICS: TO BE FREE
by Van'sGuard 258

REFERENCE NOTES 260

ABOUT THE AUTHOR 261

GLOBAL COMMUNITY
COMMUNICATIONS ALLIANCE 264

SEMINARS, WORKSHOPS,
& INTERNSHIPS 272

PREFACE

This book is a compilation of articles written by Gabriel of Urantia to address the deeper issues involved within the Occupy/99% movement and to present viable solutions to creating real and lasting change. All of the articles were posted on spiritualution.org as well as being published in on-line eZines and various blogs.

In addition, there are a few articles by other authors included in the book that were originally published in the Spring 2012 issue of *Alternative Voice* quarterly periodical, entitled "Occupy! Where Do We Go From Here?"

The Photo Gallery has a collection of photographs taken at various Occupy/99% events around the country during 2011/2012, where a team from Global Change Multi-Media (a nonprofit media division, established by Gabriel of Urantia) traveled to cover the stories and support the movement.

Spiritualution – Justice to the People
spiritualution.org

All proceeds from
the sale of this book go to the
Personality Integration Rehabilitation
Program for Teens and Adults,
founded by Gabriel of Urantia and
Niánn Emerson Chase
(pirp.info)
and Avalon Gardens
agricultural internships
(avalongardens.org)

INTRODUCTION TO THE BOOK

In this book you will see me mention many times the necessity for Americans and other countries' citizens to leave the system. "The system" to me means being almost totally under the control of the 1%, and so leaving it would be to become as independent of that 1%-controlled system as possible. I tell people to leave jobs that are not serving humanity and to find jobs and careers that are, to let their conscience be their guide. It is hard to completely leave the system and be self-sustaining, to grow your own food, and have your own water source. I encourage people to join communities and start subcultures. This can be done even in large cities. But it is very difficult to get away from the electric companies and water companies without having your own land and energy sources.

In the EcoVillage that I co-founded with Niánn Emerson Chase twenty-four years ago—called Global Community Communications Alliance (GCCA), now located in Tumacácori, Arizona, on our land we named Avalon Organic Gardens & EcoVillage—we have more than one-hundred men, women, and children from all over the world who, years ago, took those first steps that eventually led them to GCCA to become part of building our subculture. Before they joined us, they may have started recycling and composting, and then carpooling, and then quitting their jobs that did not serve humanity for ones that did, or they may have started their own businesses that serve humanity.

Eventually they found us, and now we work together with all our talents and resources to help change this world.

It is my hope that this book helps you to take those first baby steps too.

— *Gabriel of Urantia*

Let's Occupy
by Niánn Emerson Chase

With the "viral" nature of the Internet, tools of connection and communication are exploding like never before, and we are witnessing people uniting in unprecedented ways to bring about change for a better world. It was through this avenue that the Occupy movement in this country was inspired by masses of citizens of several Arab countries taking to the streets in protest of governmental injustice, tyranny, and corruption. These Mideastern people have been willing to die for their demands for a more democratic state, and in some countries thousands have already died. Ironically, the Occupy movement in the U.S. is in protest of a democracy that has gone haywire and created a huge chasm between those who have the largest amount of financial control (1% of the population) and those who are increasingly losing their financial footing in the economy (the rest of the 99% of the population).

Our country's Occupy/99% movement began on Wall Street, which represents the financial bastion of the world. It is believed by many that the financial institutions—based in a compressed area on Wall Street in New York City—is where the roots of the evil that is destroying the ideals of true democracy reside. The entire world's financial system looks to the health of "Wall Street" as a determiner of the financial health of the rest of the world. And though Wall Street is considered the center and nucleus of the world's finances, what happens in other countries does indeed affect Wall Street, thus there is a co-dependency among nations that enables destructive exploitation of people and natural resources in order to make the biggest profit. As a result, all of Earth's residents are impacted by a global economy based on unethical practices that have far-reaching ramifications.

Though the Occupy/99% movement began in New York City to protest the federal government's and private financial institutions' unholy marriage, as the movement spread to other cities in almost every state of the union, so did the platform of protest expand to issues that encompass not only economic concerns but general human rights issues, or what I refer to as the "civilizing components" of society—healthcare, education, jobs, public infrastructure, arts and culture, agriculture, food distribution, the natural environment, and so on.

As the Occupy movement took hold in people's minds, hearts, and public places over the months and began to spread, in spite of the corporate-owned mainstream media basically ignoring or misrepresenting the people and the cause, city governments and police begin to crack down on the Occupiers, and thus many of the actual physical places of Occupation ("camps") are either gone or greatly diminished. So, where does that leave the Occupy movement that began in the busy hub of New York City at an actual geographic location?

Obviously the movement has to change its tactics and begin to "occupy" more permanently people's minds and hearts, taking root in their values, goals, and lifestyles. If the Occupy movement is to survive and accomplish what it started out to do—make citizens aware of the corrupt state of our democracy and incite some justified anger and action in citizens who tend to be apathetic and passive—then it has to take hold locally, in the everyday life of citizens in every area of society.

As Gabriel of Urantia points out, more of the people who have been very comfortable in their American Dream need to become Occupiers themselves, realizing that change is necessary in every area of our society in order to recreate the true ideals of democracy.

Though I have not actually stayed overnight at any Occupy camp (though I have attended local daytime events) or traveled far to other places for Occupy events, I identify myself with the Occupy movement and consider myself an Occupier who protests and demonstrates for the cause in my daily life.

No matter the ideology, religion, race, cultural practices, or political party of people in the Occupy movement, they need to unify in their general goals to create a more democratic society that is based on providing opportunities for all people to pursue having decent lives of good health, some degree of prosperity, and the chance to pursue happiness. Thus the challenge of the movement is to attain unity without uniformity.

Interestingly, almost 150 years ago, spiritual leader Mary Baker Eddy, who founded Christian Science, encouraged people to be "occupiers" of the world, being citizens who actively promoted a healthier, more compassionate and just society. She appealed: "Occupy" until the better way comes and "be not weary in well doing." She encouraged that if their "endeavors were beset by fearful odds," and if they received "no present reward," to not go "back to error" nor "become sluggards in the race." She referred to this struggle for better ways of living as a "battle" and said that "when the smoke of battle clears away, you will discern the good you have done." She emphasized reform in individuals in order to bring about reformation in society.

We do not have to be Christian Scientists in order to appreciate what Ms. Eddy advocated in her own version of an occupy movement in her generation. We too can occupy our times in a more proactive and progressive manner by being part of the Occupy/99% movement of this generation, ever expanding our minds and opening our hearts to embrace new ways of living and working together for a truly just and humane life for all the world's citizens. It takes action—not just words—to occupy anything, and we need to do just that: occupy our world.

This article was originally published in the Spring 2012 issue ("Occupy! — Where Do We Go From Here?") of the Alternative Voice *quarterly periodical*

Niánn Emerson Chase is a descendant of Ralph Waldo Emerson, a great American activist, social commentator, writer, and a friend of Henry David Thoreau—who was famous for his solitary time spent at Walden Pond (from which he wrote the book Walden *that inspired people of the local communities to appreciate and protect the natural world) and his renowned essay Civil Disobedience (that still activates people to stand up to wrongdoing through united action). Niánn is the Co-Founder of Global Community Communications Alliance, one of the largest EcoVillages in the United States, and an author of many published articles on women's rights and other spiritual and social issues.*

Any people anywhere, being inclined and having the power, have the right to rise up and shake off the existing government and form a new one that suits them better. This is a most valuable, a most sacred right—a right which we hope and believe is to liberate the world.

~ Abraham Lincoln

We the people are the rightful masters of both Congress and the courts, not to overthrow the Constitution but to overthrow the men who pervert the Constitution.

~ Abraham Lincoln

Propaganda isn't just lies. It's broadcasting truth at the wrong time to hide what's really important.

~ Gabriel of Urantia

Defining The Spiritualution℠ Movement—A Spiritual Revolution—In Reference To The 99% Movement And Occupy Wall Street. What The People Must Do To Win Over The Power Elite

Firstly, whenever the poor and disenfranchised—who were abused for years—took to the streets, they were hosed, attacked by the police dogs, beaten with sticks, and pepper sprayed. But now this new 99% movement is not just a movement of poor blacks or other minorities but a combination of white and black races as well as yellow, brown, and red. It is a true racial coalition that has representation from 99% of the population.

Now the children of the once middle-class parents are speaking out and protesting because they have huge student loans to pay off and cannot get jobs. Where were they when they were not as much affected by the greed and power control of the elite?

People need more money because they live unsustainably. You would be surprised how cheaply you can live by practicing common-sense sustainability. The 99% movement has to become synthesized in moral and sustainable standards and adopt those higher standards themselves so that they can "sell" it to the rest of America and the world.

As Gandhi (and many other true change agents of history who have also been spiritual voices for humankind) said, "You have to be the change." The millions of India did not listen totally to him. As a result, the country was split into two countries—India and Pakistan—and are bitter enemies. Both countries have become all about the dollar bill and materialism, as most countries are. So, even though the English government conceded power to the native Indians, it still holds control over India and Pakistan through their own corporate form of Wall Street.

Writing new policies that our governments should adopt—like campaign reform, universal healthcare, and universal education—would be just the beginning of making substantial and much-needed change. But none of these bills that the 99% movement may get passed will work unless there is a universal Spiritualution movement, a change of consciousness, by the tens of thousands and millions in the 99% movement themselves, because the power elite will not let go of their dio (evil) power easily. They can only be defeated by a higher moral force or a national moral consciousness, a Deo (Godly/goodly) power, and then hopefully an international moral consciousness.

A bill passed will not change the consciousness of a people. People cannot be forced by law to totally obey a dictum by the state. The Emancipation Proclamation freed the slaves, but for more than one hundred years after that proclamation, the majority of the whites still looked at the blacks as inferior, because the whites themselves were morally inept and taught racism to their children through their outspoken beliefs, racist laws, and brutal treatment of "those of color."

If the state does adopt a moral dictum or law, people may seem compliant publicly, but privately they will still rebel against a correct legislative moral bill. They will rebel against a higher moral standard that they themselves have not risen to in consciousness.

We cannot divorce the Creator from this 99% movement. We must bring the Creator in more, because the Creator—in the consciousness of sentient freewill beings—is the author of moral standards. Moral standards are the first step towards spiritual consciousness, but the soul and mind must go further. The Creator does not want you to obey any of His commandments or moral standards just because it is the law. Many people disobey many of His commandments and moral laws, even though those standards of right and wrong are present in both the laws of the state and in their conscience.

The Creator wants you to do what is the right thing to do because you know it is the right thing to do, not because you have to do it. The Creator does not want robots in Paradise with Him. He wants a loving family who all together honor the Father who created them and each other. That is how some aspect of Paradise is created anywhere in any culture on this world. Unfortunately, many people disobey their own conscience that the Creator put in our hearts, minds, and souls to protect civilization from our lower selves.

The Creator does not want you to join a building (called a church) of dead, lifeless stones. He wants your foundations of faith to be built on the premise of love in the living waters of unity with each other. That is the "church" that Jesus was talking about.

Here is a ten-point solution to break down the unethical practices of Wall Street, the power elite, and the banks, as well as corruption in our government and injustice to the poor and disenfranchised. Basically, the whole greed-driven system needs to come down, and this is the way. Not by violence but by millions and millions of people—not only in this country but worldwide—taking part in this Spiritualution movement, a spiritual revolution and solution.

1. All citizens who work for banks must quit their jobs and trust the Creator to find them a new way of existing. They can start new businesses with others who have done the same. If the bankers have no employees, the banks will fall, and then "People's Banks" need to be formed—of the people, by the people, and for the people.

2. People who have joined the Spiritualution movement must buy land together, preferably in rural areas, with good aquifers for wells, and grow their own organic food and organic livestock (if they are meat eaters).

3. People need to stop buying the videos and going to the movies that have needless violence and thoughtless sex that make the Hollywood stars rich. By doing this, the Hollywood producers will have to change their raison d'être for making movies.

4. People need to stop going to professional baseball, basketball, and football events and paying huge ticket prices so that the so-called superstar athletes can no longer demand millions and millions of dollars while our teachers who teach our children can barely survive and often have to work two or three jobs to care for their family.

5. People need to carpool as long as gas-driven vehicles still exist and we are forced to drive them. The two-passenger-plus lanes need to become four and six lanes and have only one lane for people who drive alone. The people need to demand new forms of energy and transportation, free from the need for gasoline and oil.

6. People need to really learn how to recycle because almost everything is recyclable, with the exception of some electronic parts and toxic items.

7. People need to start building sustainably and research green building, instead of building square boxes that are fire hazards because of the materials used as well as energy-inefficient in changing seasons. This would save millions of trees.

8. People need to stop buying the products sold by corporations, particularly those that import all of their goods from overseas. If it does not say "Made in America" do not buy it. Our country was once known for some of the best products of quality on the planet. We can do that again. We need to stop being consumers of things we do not need.

Americans are addicted to shopping and usually have more clothes than they need, more shoes than they need, and too many senseless objects in their surroundings. If you do not buy the products, the corporations in America who make products overseas will come down, in other words, go bankrupt.

9. You must be aware (see Be Aware Proclamation at the back of this book) of the signs of the times, including the climate change that is causing disasters of all kinds, because if you are aware that a global shift is going to happen and that the Creator's divine hand is about to end the rebellion against His divine ordinances, you must choose sides. By doing so and having a relationship one-on-one with the Creator, you will be surprised of the peace you will have and the road of safety He will lead you down, as opposed to staying in your dreary job or imprisoning yourself in circumstances you do not really want to be in in life.

10. Pray to the Creator to lead you to elders who are true leaders. They will be concerned about the welfare of others and put your welfare before their own. They will be loving, kind, and generous, and that is how you will know who they are. You will find out that making all decisions by consensus slows down the progress of humankind. It is freedom that you crave inside, but the democracy we have now does not always work because people can very easily disobey the Constitution and other correct moral laws.

You must find people who have joined in the Spiritualution movement and come out of the fallen system. In this way, all of you will be in the divine mind together. The Creator will say the same thing to you that the Creator will say to the elder and vice versa. The elder is there to confirm the voice of the Creator inside you, concerning any matter. The Creator will talk to you first. Often you may not want to hear the voice of God inside of you, and the elder then has the responsibility before the Creator to try and guide you in the Creator's direction for you. But a true leader can use no coercion to force you to go in the Creator's direction. Unfortunately, many so-called leaders—spiritual and otherwise—use all kinds of coercion. These false leaders you must run from and not give them any power over you. But the leaders who are your fatherly examples find and treasure.

The Cry Of The Indigenous Is The Cry Of All Of Us In The 99%. What Is The Baby Boomers' And The X Generation's Responsibility?

When I was a young man in my late twenties, I went to a sweat lodge facilitated by a shaman in Pittsburgh, Pennsylvania, who was a Taino native from the tribe where Christopher Columbus landed in Central America. I told him about a book I was reading by two white Harvard graduates and pointed out a part in the book that talked about some seagulls showing up over Columbus' ship and guiding them to the landing where the Taino lived. They attributed this to Manifest Destiny—God. The shaman corrected the theory and told me that this so-called "manifest destiny," perpetrated by the white powers, meant the deaths of millions of indigenous and the suppression of them for hundreds of years until this day. I did my own research, and the shaman was correct, of course.

Those imperialists and colonizers from Europe liked to believe that God was with them as they shed the blood of the innocents throughout history. American imperialism has been no different. The power-elite had allowed for a middle class, so that the people would not totally rebel from the power-elite's greedy control. Somewhere along the way, the power-elite became so greedy that they lost sight of the fact that they could not have everybody against them, that a middle class was needed who were comfortable with a home, a car, enough money to put their kids through college, and possibly even an extra home in the mountains or a boat to take out on weekends. This is called The Great American Dream.

I was from a lower-middle-class family, born and raised in the inner city that, over the years, became more of a ghetto of racial boundaries by the time I was in my late teens. From ages one to twelve, the homes shared "party walls," where you can hear the activities of your neighbors next door, on both sides. In the back was a junkyard with rats as large as small dogs. From ages twelve to twenty-two, my very small backyard was surrounded by a saloon behind my house, a liquor store on one side, and a warehouse on the other. I knew something was wrong with capitalism when I ventured out to the suburbs or other areas of the city that were more prominent. I dreamed about living in one of those homes with a swimming pool and big yard.

Even though I had straight A's in grade school and junior high, I was not accepted in a better academic high school because the education board said my A's were "equivalent to C's" by their standards. So I was sent to an all-black high school where I was often the only white kid in my class. I got to know very well the oppression of the blacks and identified with them in many ways.

Those in the political Tea Party claim that anyone can lift themselves by their bootstraps and become "successful" in making money, maybe even becoming a millionaire. Most of those active in the Tea Party movement have never lived in an inner city ghetto or on an impoverished Indian reservation. Most "Tea Partiers" are not black or red or brown and have no idea of the struggles and oppression and marginalization still suffered by many blacks, Native Americans, or Latinos in this country. Always these people of so-called "color" have had to live with this disenfranchisement. Herman Cain, who briefly was one of the Republican candidates running for the presidency of the U.S., was the more politically-conservatives' example of a black man who had pulled himself up by the bootstraps and accomplished The Great American Dream. But Mr. Cain, on the inside, is more "white" than Ronald Reagan in his thinking, consciousness, and politics.

No matter what color individuals may be, if they are part of the power-elite—the corporate powers and the banking system that control this country and world—they are the same Christopher Columbuses that will land their ideology on the doorsteps of the marginalized people all over America and the world, because they are still looking for gold. They come in the name of peace and prosperity but want to put you and your family into bondage and slavery and rape your pocketbooks.

When the once-middle-class and their college-age children were able to obtain that Great American Dream, they did not notice and said nothing about the suffering of the marginalized, poor, and disenfranchised. Just a few of them joined the ranks of Martin Luther King, Jr. and other civil rights leaders in marches in America. Most of them sat home and watched the civil disobedience on their televisions.

Today the Occupy/99% movement is just another television show to those who are still comfortable in their American Dream, like a reality show that they can watch while they eat their dinners and drink their wine. The difference is that some of their children who cannot pay for their school loans or get jobs are on TV now, demonstrating in the Occupy/99% movement. Actually, the corporate media coverage of this movement is rare and misrepresentative, so only the parents who have learned to use the Internet or those who have satellite (and can watch alternative programs like Free Speech TV and Link TV) can see what is really happening in the Occupy/99% movement across the nation.

It is these millions of once-middle-class Americans, who still have enough money in the bank to retire, that need to really join the Occupy movement. They are definitely a part of the 99%, but they are not affected yet—just their college-age children are. Unless these Baby Boomers do what needs to be done to bring the corrupt parts of the system down, the Occupy movement will not succeed until all Baby Boomers' money is gone. And that could be sooner than they think, if a total economic collapse happens.

There is no George Bailey (played by Jimmy Stewart in the classic movie *It's A Wonderful Life*)—you know the banker who made sure all the people got their money back. No, when the banks take all your money—as the old baseball broadcaster would say—kiss it goodbye!

What Baby Boomers and some of their children who have been able to find jobs have to do now is consider quitting those jobs, if they are working for banks, weapons factories, nuclear plants, and other unethical, unsustainable companies. This will be the only thing that will bring down the greedy banking system and the military industrial complex.

Different forms of energy to power cars have been invented for years, but the powers-that-be will not let that information out and stop or slow up all production of alternative energies. Even implementing solar energy is priced so high that hardly anyone can afford to use it except those with extra money, and when the electric companies give a deal to the common man, they take half the energy for themselves. No, there has to be a national strike by people in all walks of life who work for the greedy system, for the fallen system. It does not serve humanity any longer.

All people need to see themselves as indigenous, in the sense that the issue is not a matter of black, brown, red, yellow, or white anymore; it is a matter of the "have's" and the "have-not's." The power-elite has always made it an issue of color in order to keep division among the 99%. The 1% are the puppet masters, and we all, regardless of race, have been the puppets.

I can believe in a manifest destiny led by the Creator where all people—black, brown, red, yellow, and white (a true melting pot)—are treated equally, are given free, quality education and healthcare, and who have equal opportunity to meet their God-given destiny. Unfortunately, this is the ideal manifest destiny that never ever happened in Turtle Island, called America, and in North or South America, called the Americas.

My father—who was a Marine and war veteran who fought five years in the Pacific—was a steelworker and was forced to retire in his late sixties, losing half his benefits, both financial and medical. So did thousands of other steelworkers. He worked for Jones & Laughlin. I bet you *that* family did not lose any benefits. My father died in his seventies, and my mother now is in her eighties and can only afford to live in a very small, two-room apartment in a building. My parents never owned their own home. They never had enough money to put down on one. Even under the G.I. bill, my father could not save up enough money for the down-payment. It was minimal, but to him, it took food from his two children's mouths, and he was living paycheck to paycheck. When my father died, my mother had to give up her five-room duplex in the suburbs with a nice little yard because my father's pension would not adequately take care of her bills. This happened, I am sure, to thousands of other wives of steelworkers who were also veterans of not just the Second World War but the Korean and Vietnam Wars.

We can no longer allow these kinds of atrocities to happen in America. We have to act, and we have to act now. There has to be a Spiritualution[SM] consciousness shift, meaning you have to trust the Creator to lead and guide you, once you quit those jobs that are not serving humanity in the highest way. You have to find each other and form financial support groups, communities growing your own food.

This is a revolution of consciousness, where people are waking up to the control of the power-elite over them. But the power-elite will not give up their power easily. If enough millions of people do go on strike and join the Spiritualution movement and trust the Creator to lead and guide them, a peaceful change-over of policies in this country can happen, because the power-elite will begin to lose money or they will have no employees to serve them in serfdom.

When millions of people:

- stop buying the products the power-elite sell in Wal-Mart, Best Buy, Target, K-mart, etc.
- stop buying the films that perpetuate selfishness and violence that are produced by greedy Hollywood, who pays millions of dollars to movie stars
- stop going to those concerts that make rock stars out of degenerates, drug addicts, and often not-so-talented individuals who sold out to the system to get their record contracts
- stop going to the sports events where they are paying players multi-millions of dollars when our teachers can barely survive or even get jobs

then those in power will be willing to make a deal, without Monty Hall.

The success of the many-years-old TV program "Let's Make A Deal" was based upon consumerism and people lusting for those things. Didn't the players look silly jumping up and down when they won an appliance or even a car, like an angel came down and said, "Here's the ticket to Paradise!"?

No, Baby Boomers! No, American public! No, Western civilization! It is time for a real change to happen. No President is going to do it for us. We have to do it, millions of us, everywhere. And it can start with you when you really ask the Creator to be your conscience, your friend, and your guide. Go on strike!

Lest we forget: "In God We Trust" is the United States' official motto.

Pseudo-Activism
And University Students.
The Great American Dream Is Over, But Many Millions Of Americans Still Hang On To False Hopes. The 99% Are Beginning To Awaken To The Entrapment Of The False Powers. Is There An Answer To The Future?

One Saturday my wife and I were driving to the Occupy movement in Tucson, Arizona that was going to march to the Bank of America to protest. My son and two daughters were there already, as well as several others from our intentional community. We drove past the University of Arizona stadium where the Wildcats football team was playing that day. We saw hundreds of college students walking with six-packs in their hands. As we drove by the university stadium parking lot, we saw thousands of students with kegs of beer and booths, all getting drunk and boisterous.

I thought this looked more like Sodom and Gomorrah than a university parking lot, even if there was a football game going on. But the main thought I had was these college students should be going to the Occupy Bank of America march. When we got to the march, there were only about one hundred people, but there were thousands of people at the university parking lot drinking beer.

I thought back to the first day of Occupy Tucson at Armory Park when we went there a few weeks before. While we were there, we saw several hundred university students marching in, chanting, "We are the 99%." They marched through the park and basically out the other side, returning to the university and their usual hangouts. I do not know if any of them talked to anyone at the Occupy Tucson event, and I doubt if any of them put up a tent in Armory Park and stayed there to occupy it. Many of these students probably were the same students drinking beer in the university stadium parking lot.

I realized that these students still have The Great American Dream. They have not yet graduated from college and tried to get jobs in their career choices. They are still being mostly supported by their parents—the same parents that I wrote about in another article who need to unoccupy their couches and go on strike themselves from jobs and careers that do not serve humanity. Although these students who marched in Tucson said that they "are the 99%"—(and in fact they will be, if they ever graduate, because it all may come down like Humpty Dumpty sooner than they think)—they are really part of the 1% in their consciousness, because the majority of them are part of an educational system owned and operated by the powers-that-be who feed the students the power-elite's doctrines of greed and prosperity.

Although these students are aware that graduates who went before them have huge loans they cannot pay off because they cannot find work, these current students think that by the time they graduate everything is going to be hunky dory. So with their parents' money, they can still buy all of the gadgets, drink all the beer, and go to all the bars that sell them the false message of "the good life," of The Great American Dream, that they might never realize. That Great American Dream was opportune for periods up until the 1960s.

In the beginning of our nation, immigrants were welcome, and they came from all over the world to try to build a better life, earn a decent wage to support their families, and maybe even buy a home instead of renting one. That opportunity to earn a decent wage has been gone for decades now for still too many, and it is getting worse. And gone too is the welcoming of immigrants who want to improve their lives in this country.

Most students today have a different Great American Dream. The idea of "prosperity" for the beginning immigrants—even up until the 1920s and 1930s in this country—was a lot more humble. To them, earning enough wages to feed and house their children, and maybe even send them to college, was the Great American Dream. Today, in the twenty-first century, these university students think they can be another Steve Jobs and Bill Gates and Joe Firmage. What they do not realize is those days are over for most, and the millions of poor and disenfranchised marching on the streets now—the working class, even the unions—are tired of being held captive in their dreams and ambitions and even in the ability to take care of their own families, who are now losing their homes, and many even having to live on the streets.

This dichotomy of consciousness is actually a revolution of consciousness that will divide this country into two factions: the haves and the have-nots. Malcolm X predicted this in the 1960s. All over the world the separation of consciousness between the haves and the have-nots is happening.

There have been revolutions of the people against the elite for centuries, in France and in Russia and in China and in Spain. But no system was really found to be put in the place of capitalism. So revolutionaries modified capitalism or did away with it completely and adopted communism, which was never going to work because they left out the Creator.

Jesus was a working man, a carpenter. He taught true communism, which is actually communal living and sharing, based upon being guided and protected by true spiritual leaders, who were then called apostles and disciples. This meant that these guides had a relationship with the Creator. There is a line in the book of Acts that says the followers of Jesus all went house to house and broke bread together and had all things in common. This one line, if truly followed, would be the answer to most of the problems in the world, for it says in the beginning of the Old Testament in the book of Genesis be thy brothers' and sisters' keeper.

The philosophy of many Republicans and those in the Tea Party movement is just the opposite of what Jesus taught (even though some may call themselves "Christians"). They teach instead the ideology of rugged individualism, which includes the idea that "You can pull yourself up by your own bootstraps," and the Protestant work ethic of touting that everybody who really tries can succeed and be financially prosperous and those who are not prosperous are lazy and deficient in some way. These teachings of self-reliance worked only for short periods in the beginning of American history because there has always been a gap between the rich and the poor due to many factors that include prejudice, unfairness, and greedy manipulation of circumstances and laws.

Today the gap is 1% rich and many of the 99% unable to even get a job or are on a job where their wage will never increase to really be equal to meet their own dreams of having a better car or even a boat or traveling or buying better clothes. No, they have settled for mediocrity. In their 9-to-5 jobs, many are miserable. They do the same routine everyday—come home from work, become couch potatoes, and listen to Big Brother tell them what to buy, what drugs to take (because whether they know it or not they are sick), and other propaganda to keep them happy slaves—a self-delusional existence all perpetrated by the 1% who control the masses.

The police and even the military are the slaves and the puppets of the power-elite. They have believed the lies fed them, and so they have settled for much less than what their God-given destinies could be had they become really in touch themselves and developed a real relationship with the Creator instead of the gods of propaganda in the television shows, movies, and radio programs they are mesmerized by.

Many of those soldiers who have been in the wars and somehow survived and come home to America know they were used by someone, and they come to learn that it is their own government. Many of them have even come to understand that the government is controlled by the 1% power-elite. A lot of soldiers enlist in the military and re-enlist because they have no future in the present economy, and that is just the way the power-elite wants it.

The more individuals have to depend upon the system of greed and avarice for their basic needs and to obtain some of their wants, the more they become slaves to those who will control them for the rest of their lives. Many have to sign their life away to obtain those things by loans and credit.

Even though the elite often use the words "democracy" and "freedom" in justifying their positions of unethical power and abuse, too many of the people really live in bondage and hopelessness to ever achieve their real dreams, which most shove to the back of their minds and hearts.

You do not have to be a multi-millionaire to be in the 1%. If your consciousness is that of greed and avarice, you are of the 1%. It is a consciousness too. That is why I coined the phrase "Spiritualution—a spiritual revolution," a revolution of consciousness. A personal relationship with the Creator is the only thing that can bring true justice to the people and true freedom.

If a Spiritualution[SM] consciousness shift happens on a global basis, the planet can come into the first stage of light and life, which is also called a global Divine Administration. The people of the world need to come into the divine mind, the divine mind of unity and cooperation, and care for one another. People need to grow community gardens together. People need to stop being mere consumers and live in earth harmony with all of the Creator's creation—human, animal, plant, and mineral.

If this does not happen now on a massive scale, if people all over the world do not replace the governments of totalitarian rule and dictatorship and imperialism and capitalism with a Divine Administration of true godly leaders, our earth and the people on it will perish, for we have come to the depletion of our natural resources. No man or woman has the answer, only the Creator does, and all people have to be guided by the Creator and not by the doctrines of religions or the voices of propaganda perpetrated by the power-elite in all media.

True Godly leaders do exist, but you will not see or hear them on television right now or in the movies or on the radio, for these are all controlled by the power-elite, by the gods of greed. But you can look for these true Godly leaders, because they are out there, all over the world, humble men and women who have a true concern for the welfare of not only their immediate families but for the people and children of the earth. It is these leaders you must follow—not the voices of power, wealth, and fame, but the voices of caring for one another, the true mothers of the world who nourish and comfort and the true fathers of the world who protect and guide.

You do not need a degree, certificate, or wealth to be successful and survive in this world. You need to learn to use your talents to serve others. In this manner the Creator will give you back everything you need and a hundred times more.

The Occupy Movement In Relationship To George Washington, The Colonists, And How They Won The Revolution

The Occupy movement—no matter how many protestors—is overpowered by the might of the power-elite's police force and "weapons of gas-destruction" against the poor and disenfranchised, students, and the once middle class, as the early colonists were by the British empire.

Long before the first shot was fired at Lexington—the shot heard 'round the world that it seems history does not claim was fired by either side, albeit eight colonists were killed and ten wounded while only one British soldier was wounded—or the Boston Tea Party occurred, Americans were meeting in all thirteen colonies to discuss what to do about the oppression by the British Empire over the Americans. And they met in churches, and many of those pastors became the first organizers of civil disobedience. The Americans began to show dissent on the streets in all thirteen colonies, and the unrest soon got back to the crown in England—the power-elite of that day.

Let us hope that the first shot is not fired in the Occupy Wall Street movement, because the people do not want civil war with arms in America. They just want justice to the people. Unfortunately, the first shot was fired in the Revolutionary War, and reprisals and the armed war were unstoppable, because the British Empire was unwilling to change and give justice to the people.

And so the Revolutionary Army had to be formed and organized and use different tactics to survive. And they had to find a leader to lead them. George Washington was chosen by the existing delegates of all the states of the colonies because of his military experience and the fact that he was a man who recognized the importance of the Creator's guidance in his life and in military tactics.

As all good generals understood throughout history—from Akhenaten of Egypt to David of Israel to Alexander the Great to Constantine to Oliver Cromwell of England to the Founding Fathers of America—they had to take guidance from the Creator or a higher power other than themselves. Washington, listening to the Creator, decided on hit-and-run tactics. He understood that the British were too strong to fight like they fight, two opposing forces charging against each other in open fields. The British had better training, better weapons, and longer bayonets. So Washington prayed to the Creator and came up with the same Spiritualution^{SM} principles to win the war that I am about to share with those who read this article.

Washington got together with his men and prayed with them before all battles. The men prayed daily at Valley Forge with Washington, to get them through the harsh winter. Men of all walks of life—farmers, business men, tradesmen, blacksmiths, bakers—with the pastors (many of whom were also in arms) prayed for guidance. Washington told his men to hide behind trees and huge rocks and to disappear like ghosts.

Now the Occupy movement is trying to make a statement, and the movement has to remain passive, without weapons of course. But they still have to do several things with the hit-and-run maneuvers.

Spiritualution Tactics Of Washington Against The British

1. Washington and his strategic organizers, the night before any confrontation, met and prayed and planned where the colonists would present themselves the next day in various locations, instead of one central location. This would separate the British Army and weaken their strength.

2. The next day, the organizers met with the Revolutionary Army in one central location in the morning and prayed together and then gave the orders where to occupy. They had alternate places for each confrontation location in case they had to retreat.

3. When the British soldiers came to those locations, the colonists, if overpowered, left if too many colonists were wounded or killed. They could never beat back the British by yelling and trying to scare the British off, for the British were there to beat them with the sticks, pepper spray, and gas of the day, which was the British long rifles and cannons. The colonists went to the next location separately and not in a line, as to not give attention to where they were going. Some even went the opposite direction together to be seen, therefore throwing off the British by decoy.

4. The King and Queen of England and the power-elite there felt that they were safe in their castles and mansions and their hundreds of thousands of acres, but the poor people of England (and France), by the thousands, who identified with the colonists of America, demonstrated outside the gates of the castles and mansions, without going onto the privately-owned land—just close enough to make a noise and to make the occupiers' presence known. They did not block the elites' entrance in or out, as this was civil disobedience and peaceful at all times. They did not give the elite an excuse to use violence. The poor people understood that the British soldiers might shoot anyway, and the poor had runners and couriers there to report to newspapers any violence to them by the British soldiers. Unfortunately, in their day they did not have cell phones handy with cameras and videos, and even Ustream. But they did have a global consciousness of the sufferings of other peoples in other countries, just like the Occupy movement all over the world has today for their planetary brothers and sisters.

If you do a study of the Founders of our country, you will come to the conclusion that all of them had some kind of relationship with the Creator. There were Free Masons, Protestant denominations, and even Catholics (which most history books do not acknowledge). When they wrote letters to each other—which was the method of communication in those days—the colonial delegates always invoked the Creator in some way. They may have had different opinions in the political realm, but they were of the same divine mind on things of importance when it came to the betterment of humanity as a whole. Thus the United States Constitution was written for the common good of all people, and those people included Moslems, Buddhists, Hindus, Native Americans, and people of all religions, even though the framers of the Constitution were mostly of the Christian persuasion. They did not have the vision yet of a united planetary government, but they knew that there needed to be religious freedom in the new country they were forming.

Many of them had been through the abuse of authority in Europe by religions and the powers-that-be back then. The framers of the Constitution did not leave out the Creator as a fundamental denominator in their decision making, when it came to serving the people. That is why our country became great. And people came here from the four corners of the earth for religious freedom to worship the Creator as they saw fit.

The power-elite have gradually, from the beginning of our country, tried to control the masses by bringing in Godless tyranny behind the scenes, trying to control as many of the masses as they could. Today they are the 1%, and the people are the 99%.

The 99% has to adopt the simple message of radical unity under one Creator, because we are of "One Creator, One Planetary Family." If the masses do not reconnect with their Creator individually, they will not win this revolution in trying to change corrupt and evil systems. The 99% need the

Creator's assistance—this is what George Washington knew, the delegates of all the colonies knew, and the common people of the day knew—or the movement will fall to the wayside, just like the peace movement did in the 1960s. Many of them became YUPPIES and entered the Great American Dream again, because enough of them did not trust in the Creator for guidance.

What the Occupy movement lacks today are true Godly leaders, who gather the people to pray for guidance. Without these kinds of leaders, the movement will fail just like the peace movement in the 1960s fell to greed and fear, because only faith can overcome fear and only charity can overcome greed. And both of these attributes can only be found in a relationship with the Creator.

I am not saying that there are not good people in the Occupy movement. But many a good person has lost heart and purpose without a higher vision and the Deo (Godly) power of the Creator to sustain them through difficult times of suffering that comes in all forms—some man-made by the powers-that-be against the poor and disenfranchised and now the crying-out middle class, some by the effects of global warming that is causing worsening weather patterns and other changes all over the world mostly due to corporate greed and unsustainable practices that are causing severe damage to the earth's atmosphere, water, and soil.

These are the times spoken of by many prophets of old concerning what Jesus referred to as the separation of the good seed from the bad seed. And when it comes right down to it, there are those who are more good and there are those who are more bad, and people who are more good usually have a connect with a higher power than themselves. Although they may not call that higher power "God" or "Creator," they have a connect to something other than themselves nonetheless, and they try to do what is right in their decision making for humanity, not just for themselves. This is the separation I am talking about and the separation that Jesus spoke to His apostles about concerning these days of the times of trouble on this earth.

George Washington, Thomas Jefferson, Benjamin Franklin, all the delegates, the framers of the Constitution, and the pastors of the churches of the colonies all knew that they and the people had to have a connect with the Creator to win the Revolutionary War against the government of England that had lost its connect as well as those people who profited from England's imperialism and were proud of the fact that "the sun never sets on the British Empire."

What we need to accomplish today is a world with no borders, where nationalism is not idealized and patriotism is not just towards a country or one flag, unless that flag represents all the peoples of the planet, because we need to all come to the place where we understand that there is "One Creator, One Planetary Family." We have to get bigger than just making changes here in our own country. The poor, disenfranchised, suffering peoples of the whole world are crying out for justice. We have to think bigger than just being a citizen of the United States, for we are citizens of the world.

George Washington and the framers of the Constitution believed this new country was the beginning of the New Order of the Ages. Now we have to take it to another level of consciousness and join our voices and hearts with the people of the world who cry out for true freedom and become a Divine New Order, under one Creator, coming out of antiquated evolutionary religions and dogmas and taking the exciting adventure of listening to the voice of the Creator—rather than the voice of the corporations, the corporate-owned media and false journalists, and the sold-out celebrity and sports stars—and find your destiny in the Creator's guidance.

The Occupiers Must Learn How To Use The Creator To Win Over The Power-Elite And Their Soldiers Of Gas-Destruction

History does not talk much about it (with the exception of the Old Testament and other holy writings of various religions), but most of the prophets and holy men of old have been revolutionaries, including Jesus Christ. Even over the last few centuries, revolutionaries like George Washington, Joseph Smith (of the Mormons), and Gandhi were men who prayed to the Creator for guidance. When they did pray, many of their historical accounts said that miracles happened.

From Joseph to Moses to David to Jesus to more contemporary revolutionaries and activists like Fathers Daniel and Philip Berrigan and Father Oscar Romero of San Salvador, men of spiritual power were a voice of the people of their day, and many small and large miracles happened around them.

Joseph of Israel was thrown into a well by his brothers and left for dead. He prayed for his life, and an unexpected caravan came by and pulled him out of the well. He was brought to Egypt and imprisoned, but because he had the ability to interpret dreams because of his connect with the Creator, he was called upon by Pharaoh to interpret his dream. Joseph's interpretation saved Egypt from famine, and Joseph was put second in command to Pharaoh of Egypt.

Moses was put in a basket as a baby and floated down the Nile. He could have ended up anywhere, but he ended up floating to the Princess of Egypt's palace. He could have rolled over into the water and drowned, but some guiding hand obviously was with him. The Princess raised him as her own with her other son who became Pharaoh, and Moses, the adopted son, became second also in command of the Egyptian armies. We all know of the many miracles attributed to Moses. But even if many of them did not happen exactly like the Old Testament says, something supernatural happened, because Moses was thrown out of Egypt when it was found out that he was of Jewish descent and that he killed an Egyptian soldier. He returned to Egypt forty years later and freed the Hebrew people from bondage. The most important point to be made here is that he was a man of prayer, and, according to the Old Testament, the Ten Commandments were entrusted to Moses to give to the Hebrew people.

David of Israel was a shepherd, small in stature but with tremendous faith in the Creator. He volunteered to fight the enemy giant of a soldier, called Goliath, in a one-on-one battle, and David had only a slingshot. According to the Old Testament, David said, "You come against me with your strength, your sword, and shield, but I come against you with the power of the Creator." (These are my words, but that is close enough, because what actually was written was, "I come against you in the name of the God of Israel.") Saul—one of the power-elite of his day as the King of Israel—tried to kill David because Samuel the Prophet said that

David would be king one day. Saul, with all of his army and local police force, could not murder David because David was destined to become king. When David did become king, he was the people's choice for king (besides the Creator's), and David brought prosperity to Israel as he served the people through his office. There were no separations at that time between the 1% and the 99% in that country any longer. David considered himself one of the 99%.

Moving up to the 13th century, Francis of Assisi, as a warrior-soldier, was captured by the enemy and became a prisoner of war. While in prison, he had a spiritual experience with the Creator. He was from a very wealthy merchant family, and, after his encounter with the Creator, he left his father's wealth and became a poor brother monk and worked with the poor and disenfranchised of his day. Unlike David, Francis led no army of arms, but before he died thousands of Franciscan followers became his little brothers, and they changed the history of the Catholic Church and the Catholic Church's work with the poor and disenfranchised.

Oliver Cromwell, one of the 99% in the seventeenth century—who was called "Lord Protector" of the people—started a revolutionary army against King Charles I, the 1%, and won against the King's larger and better-trained army. He did this through personal prayer and by praying with the people and by hearing from the Creator the tactics to win against the power-elite of his day. When he won, he formed a Parliament of the people and of the 99%, just like the Founding Fathers of America began their federation of 99%-ers.

We all know the story of George Washington and how he won over the British empire, whose military imperialism conquered the whole known world at that time with British might and power. In history books it is said that George Washington was shot many times but did not die, although the wounds he suffered would have killed most other men. In one battle alone he had four bullet holes in his jacket and miraculously no scars on his body. The protection from the divine can be just as real today for the 99% as it was for the colonists who fought against the might of the British empire, but it cannot be done without prayer and faith.

In modern times, Nelson Mandela was put in prison for twenty-seven years, tortured in his younger years, put into solitary confinement, starved, and separated from family and friends, with no visitors. How did this man deal with this isolation and suffering all these years? He said he dealt with it by prayer. How did this man of simple faith, who had no voice for all those years, eventually gain release from prison and shortly thereafter became president of South Africa? He would be the first to tell you: by prayer and the will of the Creator.

The reason I tell all these stories of men and leaders of great faith is because it would take men and women—by the thousands and millions—of great faith and various degrees of faith in the Creator, who pray for answers and miracles, to win over the awesome imperialistic power worldwide of the power-elite and the 1% who control the masses of people all over the planet. Without the Creator's help, there can be no victory.

Like Gandhi and Martin Luther King, Jr. (another holy man), I believe in passive resistance, civil disobedience, and peaceful demonstrations. But even in these non-violent methods of revolutionary tactics, people must still hear from the Creator, like Martin Luther King, Jr. did, to make the kinds of changes that the Civil Rights movement was able to make. Although Martin Luther King, Jr. was killed by an assassin's bullet, his voice was not silenced, because now there were millions of voices all crying out for freedom. They may have murdered the man, but they could not murder the movement.

In the Occupy movement today there are many leaders, leaders who are organizing in cities all over the world. It is not really a leaderless movement. On the contrary, it is a movement of hundreds of leaders all over the world and millions of individuals—call them soldiers for freedom, call them voices crying out in the wilderness, but you cannot call them hippies or drug addicts or freeloaders. No, on the contrary, they are people who want to work. They are people who want equal opportunity. They are people who are beginning to see the light and the oppression that the power-elite has over them and their once-middle-class parents, even though those parents may not see this oppression themselves.

This Occupy movement is making leaders out of former university students, union workers, school teachers, and people from all walks of life, just like the Civil War made leaders out of former slaves. And those slaves helped to end the power-elite's stranglehold on the blacks of their day. The slaves of today's America and other countries in the world are speaking out against the slave owners today. The difference is the slaves today are white, black, yellow, red, and brown all over the world.

Here in America the power-elite is still in control of the media, television, and movies, so we are fed *Entertainment Tonight* and *Extra* and other decoy entertainment that is really propaganda to tell the American public, "Look everything's OK. You can have these riches too. You can be famous too. You can have these jewels too, just like Elizabeth Taylor." We see the lifestyles of the rich and famous, and we are told to desire what they have and that we can have it too. What they do not tell you is that you have to sell your soul to get it. And many many do sell their souls to get it, not caring who they hurt to get it or who they step on, as long as they get it.

There is no college course called "Manifesting 101." Instead we have to take courses like Business 101, Economics 101, and Marketing 101, and we begin to learn the line that Michael Douglas said in his first *Wall Street* movie, "Greed is good." We learn the art of manipulation, because any art is a practiced discipline, and with manipulation, over time, you can become really good at it, and deception is manipulation's tool. Unfortunately when you practice manipulation too much, you can never leave it at the office or workplace. You take it home with you, and you use it in your family life, with your friends, and before you know it you are on your fourth marriage, and although you might have "succeeded" in your pursuit of materialism and financial success, you are a failure in being a loving husband and father and have probably no real friends at all, because you lost them climbing that ladder of success.

There is a true way to manifest one's destiny. There is a true way to manifest all the needs that one needs in one's life and the lives of your children and grandchildren. But you could not even begin to see how this works until you begin to practice it yourself. Just like you practice being a manipulator, you must practice being selfless. When you set that law in motion in the universe, the Creator then begins to act for you. It is a beautiful and serendipitous way that the Creator reveals Himself to you, to groups, and to governments. When you pay it forward to others, the Creator pays it forward to you. This is the only way that our world will change, and the common folk all over the world are beginning to do this, some first with baby steps within the Occupy movements everywhere. They are taking care of one another. They are donating to the cause, and this cause is the cause of true freedom. And it has just begun.

Capitalism cannot be replaced with socialism or any other form of government. It is going to take millions and millions of people all over the world coming into a personal relationship with the Creator and coming out of antiquated religions and organized denominational and nondenominational churches and coming into the same divine mind that all of the Creator's children must be able to hear from. One article alone cannot begin to teach what a planetary Divine Administration would be like. But this Spiritualution[SM] teaching must begin within the 99%. (spiritualution.org)

Jesus said that we have to be in the world but we do not have to be of the world. "No one can serve two masters: for either he will hate the one, and love the other; or else he will hold to the one, and despise the other."[1]

The 99% are finding out what many spiritual people throughout history have found out, that you cannot serve God and the power-elite at the same time. It is not that those in the 99% movement do not want to work. They do not want to work any longer for the puppet masters. As a matter of fact, people all over the world need to go on strike if they are working for the power-elite. That is how to bring them down. Employees all over the world need to quit their jobs at General Electric, Goldman & Sachs, Target, Wal-Mart, all of the oil companies, all of the big greedy banks, insurance companies, nuclear weapons factories and power plants, Proctor & Gamble, NBC, ABC, CBS, Fox, CNN, Time-Warner, Cox, Microsoft, Google, Verizon, Apple, and many, many more. Do not think that your job is respectable any longer.

Doctor Albert Schweitzer (and many doctors like him) left the 1% to serve humanity as missionaries to the poor and disenfranchised in Africa. He did not go to work in a prestigious hospital or any other form of prestigious medical work. The going-on-strike theme within the 99% movement has to expand to the people who have "respectable" jobs, because they are no longer respectable when you help to keep afloat the 1%'s powerful organizations.

No, you need to desire to serve humanity, and you need to trust the Creator to lead and guide you where He wants you to serve humanity. You must have the same faith as Joseph of Israel, as Gandhi, and as Martin Luther King, Jr., and say no to the system that works only for the 1% rather than for the 99% of the world.

The Higher-Consciousness-Handicapped Presidential Nominees, Our Current Compromising-Consciousness President, And The Need For Both To Lean On Somebody Or Fall

The Republican nominees who ran for the presidential candidacy in 2011 and 2012 can also be called "the parade of new souls." There is a lot to learn about the difference between a new soul and an older soul or starseed, which has taken me authoring two published books (called *The Cosmic Family, Volumes I* and *II*) so far to even begin to teach. But for the clarity of this article, I will just state a few pertinent facts on both soul types. The majority of the billions of people on this planet are new souls, but there are approximately 500 million starseed over the age of eighteen who are older souls and many under eighteen.

The new souls are mostly in error with a lot of their thinking, because they simply do not have the astral (past-lives) experience of an older soul. That is why so many new souls become fundamentalists in their thinking. To them, everything is either black or white. Fundamentalists usually are very "right" or extremely conservative in their political and social views and are not open-minded enough to see enough alternative opinions.

They dogmatically read scriptures as if every written sentence is absolute truth, without contemplating other scriptures about the same subject or even updated scientific facts about the same subject. Not that science is always right either, but new souls who are fundamentalists usually take things at surface value when it comes to scripture interpretation. So they have become known to us here in America as "evangelicals" and basically think everybody else in the world is going to hell because the others do not believe in their form of religion—basically that people need to be "washed in the blood of Jesus."

It does not matter if others believe in the crucifixion and resurrection of Christ and believe that He is coming again. To the Christian fundamentalist a person has to believe that Jesus shed His blood for the sins of mankind, and that He was the sacrificial lamb of God who takes away the sins of the world. And so to them, a lot of other denominational Christians are not "saved" either, and neither are Moslems, Hindus, Buddhists, Jews, or New Agers. That is why evangelicals and those leaning toward the political right are ready to start a war with Iran and billions of other Moslems, because to the fundamentalists the Crusades are not over yet, and it will culminate at Armageddon. (Actually, to the Moslem fundamentalist, the Crusades are not yet done either.)

Christian fundamentalists need the Bible, particularly the New Testament, as a crutch to lean on. Let me explain by using an analogy. I inherited diabetes from my parents' and grandparents' genetics. It has taken its toll on my physical body. I have lost sight in an eye, had to have a kidney transplant (after being on dialysis for 8 months), gotten neuropathy in my legs and feet (which makes me imbalanced when I walk), and to top it off, I fell and fractured my hip and an orthopedic surgeon put a titanium rod in my right leg, which shortened it one inch, causing me to limp. So I need a cane to lean on. I often have to use a railing or someone's arm to lean on. Without that, I definitely would walk lopsided and off balance or fall.

Fundamentalist Christians are very off balance when they lean on their narrow-minded interpretations of the Old and New Testaments (that they inherited from previous fundamentalists), particularly the New Testament, which they think is the final word from God. It does not matter that it is 2,000 years old and no longer "new" at all. The point is, this is the mindset of those who want to lead our country and have led it. They refer to the scripture verses as a solemn foundation of their faith when they should be referring to the love, joy, peace, patience, and kindness and all the other virtues that Christ talked about. They are mostly in error, and error is evil. And the results are harmful to individuals and masses.

The older souls, like President Obama, are more sophisticated in their sin. And sin is knowing it is wrong but doing it anyway—compromising. Older souls have learned to lean on their wit, their manipulation ability, because they can manipulate most others. Both new souls and older souls manipulate the public. Newer souls are more blatant about it and do it with a smirk on their face (like Bush had), that says, "I just don't give a care; I'm doing it my way," whereas older souls manipulate with more sophistication. The public even likes them for it, because they are so smooth. But they can only get away with that manipulation for so long, and they too will be found out. The starseed or other older souls who voted for them once will not vote for them again.

When he was first elected, President Obama had a chance to really do some good for this country and had millions of people behind him. But he chose the way of compromise, and he compromised with the more iniquitous. The corporations and their executives are iniquitous, and iniquity is not caring who you hurt for the sake of personal gain and profit.

Both new souls and older souls can compromise wrongly, and this has been a problem in our country since the beginning of the Constitution and the proper interpretation of it. Basically, today, both parties compromise with the corporations' iniquitous executives. Obama's platform was making "change you can believe in." But just about everything he did when he became President, no one believed in—certainly not the people who voted him in, just the corporations. Instead of giving hope of a better life for all, like he promised, he gave the American people continued oppression and suffering.

Now maybe he does not see it this way. That is because when you compromise, you become blind to seeing what you need to see. And then it is the blind leading the blind, until enough of the blind people wake up. What the majority people need to wake up to this time is: no matter who they vote for, there will be no real change, because the existing two-party system does not work anymore and neither does capitalism.

"Money" has not worked on this planet for thousands of years, at least not the way it should have worked for "the common good of all." The use of money has caused feudalism, dictatorships, plutocracies (government by the wealthy), oligarchies (government by a few elite families), and capitalism. But no matter what you call it, it is government based upon greed, profit, and selfishness, and usually the profit ends up in the hands of the few.

Older souls should have the experience to do the right thing, but they may not have the moral fiber to do the right thing. That is why they are still on this planet. There are many who are on this planet who are older souls and would make better presidents, but you will never hear of them, because they would not make the compromises for them to be the politicians, corporate executives, and movie stars (because these people have all had to compromise in some area of their moral life to get where they are in the fallen system).

You may call me an idealist, but I believe that we can trade services, talents of all kinds, goods for other goods, and get along just fine on this planet. There are many groups and intentional communities around the world now doing this. One such group of people in Portland, Maine are involved in Hours Exchange Portland, with approximately 750 people (and still growing), who exchange services with each other rather than money. Many of them have lost jobs and homes and are trying another way to exist in this broken economy and broken political system. They are the once-middle-class, not the poor and disenfranchised (who have always suffered from capitalism and lack of free higher education).

Through my writings and teachings for twenty-three years now, I have been telling people to leave the broken mainstream system and form communities, have all things in common (as much as you can), grow your own food, be near a good water source, and build and live sustainably. This will be a must for people to do if they want to survive in the near future, for this present system and its greed cannot last too much longer. This is why the Occupy movement is saying "we've had enough." But they are not quite sure what to do about it. Hence, I just gave the answer at the beginning of this paragraph.

The mainstream system can no longer be changed from the inside out. It has to be started all over again on a more moral and just foundation. The old order has to go and a divine new order has to come. I say divine because, as I have said in many of my teachings (including my autobiography *The Divine New Order*), you cannot leave out the Creator in your personal life or in your country's future.

Some of you might think I am going too far if I said I do not believe in nationalistic borders or countries or religions or anything that separates us from living as one planetary family, because ultimately, that is what we are—one family of the Creator, living together on one planet. Until individuals all over the world begin to see themselves as part of one planetary family—as planetary citizens, not citizens of any one country—we will continue to war, compete wrongly with each other, and not share the natural resources that this planet has to offer. When our resources run out, we will go and take someone else's, always in the name of some "noble" cause (when the real reason is oil, or water, or land, or food, or whatever we think we need).

It is a much bigger problem than just issues about healthcare, education, immigration, abortion, gay rights, energy, foreign policy, or oil. It goes all the way back to the beginning of Genesis, where it is written and said by the Creator that we need to be our brothers' and sisters' keeper. And if you are not doing this in your life, then you need to get out from under the life you are living and into a community of people where you can serve each other. This is the only way that the real change that is needed will ever come.

The Judicial System: Why It Does Not Work And How It Can. Occupy The Courts.

I was a volunteer chaplain at the Pima County Sheriff's Department. I worked at the county jail from 1977 to 1982. I also worked with the pre-trial release program of the Department of Economic Security and accepted prisoners to my halfway house, if I thought I could work with them. Many of these prisoners I got personally involved with. I went to their trials. I learned a lot about the "injustice system" because none of these prisoners had the money to really hire an attorney, so most of them had court-appointed attorneys to defend them. And a lot of those attorneys were wet behind the ears.

It is true that many prisoners are sorry they got caught but are not so sorry they did the crime. So I tried to work with the one in a hundred, who I felt was a victim and innocent of what he was charged with. Countless times I had to experience what I felt were innocent victims going to prison or being prosecuted by high-powered prosecutors in the District Attorney's office.

On the other side of the coin, I know there were many prisoners who were guilty who were set free by a jury because of the smooth-talking defender. Most of these prisoners came from families with money to hire better attorneys. Basically, what I learned very quickly is that all too often money bought freedom for the guilty and lack of money meant prison for the innocent.

So I began to see that in the criminal justice system, often the "criminals" were the attorneys and the judges, who went only by the letter of the law, because that is how they got to be judges—by compromising their integrity for position and power. Once I attended a court hearing for a mother of three children who the father had custody of. He tricked the mother into giving him custody, saying it would help him in his taxes but that they would in reality have joint custody, etc. But when he was given custody, he would not let the children see their mother, and he turned around and sued the mother for child support. The father and his new wife together made more than $100,000 at the time (and that was twenty-five years ago).

The judge's decision was for the father, who had hired a high-powered attorney. The mother had no money to hire an attorney, and since this was a civil matter, the court did not appoint her a lawyer. The judge went by the letter of the law and not by the grace of the law. The letter of the law states that a woman should also pay child support. But in this case, the father knew that the mother was not working and had quit her job to go into missionary work. This decision by the judge caused this mother no end of grief for many years. And because of the father's cruelty, he turned her three children against the mother, and she has not seen the children for more than twenty years.

In a true judicial system, that is overseen by a governing board of men and women who know the

Creator, attorneys would not have to win their cases, unless a person was really guilty or really innocent. In other words, they do not have to take a case if they are a defender and think the person is guilty. As a matter of fact, they should not take the case. The defender should only take the case if the person is innocent. That is what a defender is. A defender's job is not to get a guilty person off, like in the case of O.J. Simpson (who many think is guilty) and countless others. This is real crime. And the prosecutor should not prosecute a case if he thinks the person is innocent. He should not bring false evidence to light in the courtroom nor should the attorney use his or her smooth tongue to convict the innocent. There are many prisoners in prison who are innocent because the attorney was the criminal.

Attorneys justify themselves charging huge sums of money an hour—some $600 or $700 an hour or more—because they are white-collar criminals. They can get away with it and look good. But if they had a real true conscience before the Creator, they would not be able to do these kinds of things. These are not just attorneys of criminal law practice, they are attorneys of all kinds: family practice, immigration, First Amendment, you name it. They somehow justify their huge incomes, and the whole system is set up for the attorneys to make lots of money. So too are the laws set up for the attorneys to make money, and the attorneys make the laws! And so usually the only ones who win in the judicial system are the attorneys, and all judges were once attorneys.

Lest we forget, the judicial system is one of the branches of government, and in the Supreme Court the nine judges, who were once attorneys, have the final authority in all the cases that are brought to them. Supreme Court justices are appointed by the President (who nominates them by and with the advice and consent of the Senate) and hence they are influenced by other interests and have to compromise even more. The problem is these nine souls most of the time, for more than two centuries now, have been new souls with one lifetime of experience. Under a true Divine Administration this would never be allowed.

The need for judges has been the case ever since civilization began to develop, long before the book of Genesis was written (attributed to Moses) and long before the Pentateuch (the books of the law) was written (also attributed to Moses). Moses appointed judges for all the tribes to judge the people. Later in history, when the people cried out for a king, the king became the main judge. But other lesser judges still existed, all by the grace of the king, and if the king was a godly king, this worked out fine. If he was not, evil men became the judges and injustices occurred.

This is true down to this very day. Today, many judges should never even run for office, realizing that they cannot really make decisions for true justice, even if they win their judgeship. If they are naïve and do not know that, they find out real soon that they will not advance in the system unless they make decisions based upon the influence of corporations and money-people with private interests involved. Many judges who find this out do resign, but many do not and allow themselves to be trapped in the system of greed by compromising their own values for the sake of prestige and bigger paychecks and payoffs.

As history passed from the time of Moses down to the present age, the need for attorneys in all walks of life became the norm. The majority of these attorneys work within the corrupt system, and even if they wanted to do something right, they find out that it is very difficult because the system complements greed, money, and power—not truth, innocence, and goodness. The poor and disenfranchised have very little chance of justice in the present judicial system. That is why our prisons are full of slaves, who "work" for the owners of the privatized prisons by just even their mere presence, because each prisoner brings in a certain amount of money.

In the Old Testament is a story of two women who came before Solomon. Both of them claimed that a child was theirs, so Solomon said, "I will split the child in half and then give each mother a half." When the sword was raised, the real mother put herself between the sword and the child, and Solomon knew who the true mother was. Today, if the false mother had money, she would win custody of the child over the real biological mother. It has happened time and time again in today's courts. Fathers who are actually drug users and criminals, because they come from wealthy families, win custody over the mothers who do not have the money to hire high-powered attorneys.

Justice to the people? There is very little justice, unless you can buy it in present-day America. Money buys better education and healthcare, travel, luxury housing, and of course the subject of this article: favorable decisions in the courts. The Constitution is even interpreted wrongly by unscrupulous attorneys who make amendments to the Constitution that are criminal. They make laws that our Founding Fathers ran from in Europe. The whole reason they came to America and fought a revolution from England was to set up a Constitution of the people, for the people, and by the people.

Until we get back to that raison d'être, there will be no justice, and our present judiciary system will only be a tool for the 1%. As Moses and all the prophets of the Old and New Testaments and all the visionaries of history tried to tell the people in the renaissances of their time, without a moral standard (a Spiritualution—a spiritual revolution), the country will fall into violent revolution. Hopefully, there will never come again in this country a revolution of arms, but in order for that not to happen, more and more Americans of the once-middle-class have to wake up. The bought-and-paid for police force have to wake up, and even young men and women (and older men and women alike) in the military have to wake up, for it is by force of arms and certain laws that the 1% now control the people—it is not love and certainly not justice.

A Series Of 3 Articles On Community Building And Survival In Times Of Economic Crises

PART 1

Community Living—The Answer As To How To Defeat The 1%. The Establishment Of Subcultures.

This article is a response to a member of the arts and labor group of Occupy Wall Street, Nicole Demby, and her excellent article titled, "The Fight Against Capitalism" printed in *AdBusters*, February 15, 2012.

Throughout recorded history, and even before that, people lived in communities/tribes and had as many things in common as they could, because tribal living simply made life easier for everyone involved. It was a protection against more hostile enemy tribes as well as the 1% of their day (and there has always been a 1%, since the establishment of using some sort of capital as a means of acquiring goods and services).

The 1% have always come against communal living and people having as many things in common as they could, because people become less of consumers and do not have to interact as much with the ruling or corporate entities, past or present.

Throughout history, the establishment or bourgeoisie, as well as the controlling 1%, have always persecuted people who tried to live outside the system. They have even sent armies to destroy these villages and committed terrible atrocities towards anyone who tried to live an alternative lifestyle to what the 1% dictated. The English did this with the Scottish and Irish as well as many other peoples they colonized in other lands. Now, in the United States of America, the 1% misrepresent the alternative leaders and use the "C" word (cult) to label people who walk out of the system to form intentional communities.

Because these alternative leaders, for hundreds of years, have been persecuted, misrepresented, and even murdered, many communities began to adopt consensus rule so that these leaders would not have to meet the fate that alternative leaders would meet by leading new societies away from the system. Consensus may work in the beginning of a movement, but it would never work for long when you have over a certain amount of people trying to live and survive together, which involves the growing of one's own food, housing, transportation, communications, and—in today's society—Internet and technology.

The more people who join the intentional community (and more people are needed whenever food is grown because farming takes a lot of work and labor, as does the processing of this food and the distribution of it to the people), the more complex the challenges in maintaining that community. Families have children and the children need to be raised, and many decisions have to be made in the raising of children and their schooling. This takes leadership, because consensus can never solve the problems that develop as a community begins to grow past a dozen or so people. Decisions have to be made quickly, and consensus cannot come to conclusions quick enough.

Through the natural process of civilization growing, leaders have always risen to places of responsibility simply because they are needed, because final decisions have to be made in a sometimes immediate timetable. The communities who had strong leaders throughout history have survived the longest and became more powerful villages, and these villages and their leaders have developed into what was known as chiefs and elders, and eventually mayors, when people got more away from communal living and lived in individual housing. In every civilization that prospered there has been some form of eldership.

The kibbutzes served their revolution and the establishment of a new country, Israel, in two ways in the late 1940s. They provided necessary housing where people could live less expensively and provided a communal atmosphere to share things in common. The biggest thing that they provided was a sense of unity and purpose. In this country, the Mormons (under tremendous persecution) as well as the Bruderhof communities survived and prospered because they had all things in common and lived outside the mainstream.

In a more profound sense, all of these groups created a divine new order. "Divine" because they were living the principles that many legitimate spiritual leaders have taught, including Jesus in the first century. The first disciples of Jesus had all things in common and ate together. This is divine. It has nothing to do with being religious. It does have to do with being spiritual and really loving your neighbor as yourself and sharing what you have. In the present old order, the 1% control pretty much everything, and people have to buy it or they will not get it.

In many third-world (developing) countries, where many people could not survive under the dictatorships and abusive governments, they had to leave the system and form alternative communities to survive. This was done in Chiapas, Mexico, in Nicaragua, in Guatemala, in San Salvador, and it is done now in many African and satellite countries of the once-Soviet empire. This is what U.S. citizens have to do in the Occupy movement, and what Egyptians have to do, and what Syrians have to do, and Yemenis have to do, and what Greeks have to do.

The system that serves the 1% itself is falling down, and only the rich will survive. And those who were once middle class, who still have money in the banks, will survive for a while, until their money runs out. Only by the 99% leaving the system and forming subcultures will the 1% really be affected, because they have the might, the military, and can buy the power. The system is too corrupt to change it from within.

Alternative communities today need to become free and self-sustaining from the system. But getting off the grid is not an easy thing to do, for the 1% want people to stay on the grid. That is why solar power and other forms of alternative energy are so expensive. That is why alternative building materials are almost nonexistent, because the system wants to keep you in square boxes and build with all the corporate-controlled materials—wood, steel, plaster, and so on—to keep the people subjugated to the system.

Architects find out that it is very hard to build their dreams of beauty and sustainability in this system. They can draw the plans and have the vision, but the reality of building it is prevented by the control of the 1% in the building trades and codes. Well-known architect Paolo Soleri with his Arcosanti in Cordes Junction, Arizona has taken many decades to build by donations and with the help of other architects and students who believed in the vision and worked for nothing. But still Arcosanti is a long way from being complete.

Much work still needs to be done in Avalon Organic Gardens & EcoVillage, in Tumacácori, Arizona in Santa Cruz County—with 100+ men, women, and children from around the world—that had to move from Yavapai County because of the county restrictions and encroaching gated, expensive developments hostile to agrarian, alternative living. Many counties in the United States have codes that are anathema to true community and green building. So counties must be found with more expansive building codes and progressive thinking. Some intentional communities have even had to leave the United States for other countries to totally realize the vision of self-sufficiency and green building.

With the high cost of gasoline today, community carpooling is not only the wisest way to go but will soon be the only way to go, for few people can afford the rising cost of gasoline. And so these communities can buy passenger vans and transport twenty people to one place instead of two to four people in a car. Most Americans drive with only one in a car. On some of our highways there is a separate lane to the far left for those cars to use that have two or more people riding in them. Usually traveling in that lane is much faster because it is much less crowded. Perhaps we should make this lane available for cars with three or four people. That would be even more sustainably sane and economically wiser and would force people to be even more economically- and environmentally-minded when driving.

In the intentional community at Avalon Organic Gardens & EcoVillage, vehicles are not individually stewarded, and people share the same cars, rather than just one person having a car. Vehicles are available when the need to use one comes up. The community itself pays for upkeep of the vehicles and supplies the fuel. The ideal would be to use electric cars, when they are perfected for long-distance driving in rural areas.

Also in the community all income goes to the community, which in turn supplies all personal needs—clothing and so on—even dental care (which most insurance policies and the government do not supply to the people). Housing is owned by the community, and all houses are built within the community property. The children are privately schooled, and many of the teachers have many years of teaching experience as certified instructors. The idea is that people can walk to each other's homes and to make the environment as sacred as possible, at one with the earth.

There are many different modus operandi within different intentional communities, but basically the general principles are similar: people sharing and having more things in common than the average U.S. citizen. What are called "communities" in some U.S. cities, particularly modern condominium timeshares, are not the intentional communities I have been referring to. People do not share in these communities. They may share a common swimming pool, clubhouse, and Laundromat, but that is about it. They own their own condos and have to buy their own food and pay for their water, just like everyone else does in the established American system. No money, then no food, no electricity, no water.

If you are not a vegetarian or vegan, the raising of animals is a must for any alternative community, and so enough land has to be acquired to raise animals—cows for eating and milking, goats for milking and eating, chickens for eating and their eggs, and so on. At Avalon Organic Gardens & EcoVillage we also are starting fish hatcheries.

It takes a lot to feed 100 or more people, and any intentional community with this number of people must be near a good water source and have their own wells with good aquifers. And so investigation must be done before any land is bought, to be sure that there is an adequate water source and that the water is good.

Running a community of 50–100 people or more takes a lot of administration. People need to be appointed to lead in different areas of functions. Consensus will not work when you need to supply the food and material needs for this many people. Strong and wise leadership is the only thing that has worked in the history of communities throughout the planet. A good leader will seek the counsel of others and draw his or her conclusions from the consensus or majority of their opinions.

Because of industrialization, the majority of humankind moved from rural areas to living in densely-populated, urban areas, thus people got away from the land and sharing common things. They now buy what they need in mega-stores that are corporate-owned chains like Wal-Mart that supply most of what people need, even food. But what you cannot get in these corporate giants is a true sense of neighborhood because the small, independently-owned local neighborhood businesses hardly exist anymore. Many Americans have forgotten what a true neighborhood is.

In hospitals, too many unnecessary C-sections for convenience have taken the place of natural, vaginal births and a knowledgeable midwife. Powdered milk and other formulas have taken the place of less expensive and healthier breastfeeding.

So getting back to the land has to happen first in the consciousness, not just in the physical aspect of it. In a true neighborhood, you know your neighbors. You know them by their first names. You may not see them every day, but you may see them once or twice a week, whereas in suburban America you may not see those who live in close proximity for months or even years. Some people have lived beside someone for years and have never known their first names.

True neighbors care about each other. They make sacrifices for each other. They play together. They share with each other. They pass down their clothes to the children of other families. They eat together, maybe not every night, but in communities single people definitely like to have that camaraderie of eating together. In alternative communities the elderly are taken care of, not put in old-age homes and separated from the rest of society. The sick are cared for by the healthy in communities and not left alone and lonely. The sick know that they are cared for. When you are sick in American suburbs, you are pretty much on your own except for your immediate family, who often are too busy themselves to give you the kind of care you need (or they might not even live in the same house, neighborhood, city, or state).

Young married couples have a better chance of making it in their marriage in intentional communities, because their expenses are down to almost nothing. And they have the concern of and help in child-raising and marriage counseling by their elders that people who live in suburban or urban America do not have.

True intentional communities in America today have the best chance of breaking the yoke of capitalism. Although certain things still need to be bought in the system, the more people who join the community with right motives and purpose, the less money needed because the people bring with them their talents to contribute for the common good. And the more people who work together for a common purpose, the more that can be created for the community as a whole and the less the need to purchase anything outside of the community, therefore eventually ending capitalism (as it is today) within that society.

The consultants of Avalon Organic Gardens & EcoVillage are available for your consultation in agriculture (the process of growing and supplying food), sustainability and permaculture (learning how to live off the grid and more economically), green building (by our staff of Earth Harmony Builders), and administrative advice (how to organize and run intentional communities based upon leadership and the tribal understanding of eldership).

E-mail us at: csa@avalongardens.org

or call (520) 603-9932

PART 2

Substitutes For Community Living. Modern Society And The Breakdown Of Having All Things In Common, Including Interpersonal Relationships

With the onslaught (particularly in Western civilization) of modernization, industrialization, and technology, people have become more isolated from each other and from the local community where they may live. At one time in our human history people used to know the names of everyone in the tribe or neighborhood. They ate, played, washed clothes, watched each other's children, fixed each other's broken-down equipment, worshipped God together in kivas and outdoor arenas, helped raise the animals, and often shared the same modes of transportation (horses, chariots, wagons, etc.). The following specifics are some of the reasons why community has been lost in present-day civilization.

When the worship of God went into buildings, people lost touch with the idea of God being in nature—not that pantheism is correct, not that God lives in a tree, but the idea that God created the tree. So people's minds no longer "clicked" with the idea of God (as Creator) being in the trees, the earth, the fruits, the vegetables, and the water in creeks, lakes, and rivers. Instead, God lived in an altar inside a building. In both Catholic masses and Protestant services, the Eucharist (the bread or wafer) given at communion took the place of communal meals, of people eating together. The priest or pastor took on the role of representing God rather than people seeing God in each other because the priest and pastor became the focal point of everyone in the congregation's eyes; they were up front.

The modern laundromats—where people go and wash and dry their clothes and usually talk to no one else—as well as having a washing machine in each home, took the place of women in communities doing these kinds of things together. There was a time when many women washed their clothes in local creeks or rivers together in groups and made washing clothes a day of fun, often swimming in the creek or river and bringing their children. But today the creeks and rivers are polluted because of greed that rules industry and unsustainable development that does not have the environment or the area's residents in mind.

Restaurants emphasize the selling of served food and often do not consider a friendly environment that encourages strangers talking with each other. People today go to restaurants with one or perhaps a few other people and talk only to those in their party. Although the restaurant may be crowded, the idea is not to relate with anyone else. That is not the way of communities and tribes in the history of this planet. Eating was a time of communication with each other, of laughing, of sharing the day's experiences, of inviting strangers into the conversations and getting to know them. The art of stimulating and friendly conversation has been lost among most.

Even the beginning coffee houses—that started in Europe as places of poetry, art, music, and passionate conversation—have changed to: "Where can I get the best cup of coffee? Oh yeah, Starbucks! I can bring my laptop there and I don't have to talk to anybody." As a matter of fact, if you try to really converse with someone, they may take you the wrong way and be suspicious of your motives in trying to be friendly, so people do not even try to be friendly today. Women may think the men are trying to "come on" to them (and men vice versa) if they try to start up a conversation, because most men do not know how to be friends with women today. Thus most women do not approach men for simply friendly communication with no sexual strings attached.

People are lonely in modern civilization. You can live in a city of several million people and feel very alone, because society has grown to not trust each other or speak to each other or even care about each other. A true community of people is supposed to do all of that and more. That is what communal living is all about.

Jesus never intended for church-community gatherings to be the mega-churches of today, with thousands of people. Many of these mega-church pastors say, "Well we have group home meetings." That is a start towards community building within a huge church, but are there enough real elders to care for the spiritual and emotional needs of such a large number of people? How much did it cost to build that mega-church that seats thousands of people, even up to 10,000–15,000? Many of those mega-church gatherings have more of an emphasis on entertainment, concerts, or events like speakers who are the world's tallest Christian or the world's shortest Christian.

All people have a need for love and to be loved, to be guided and to be cared for, particularly the elderly when they get older. But today many elderly are sent to assisted-living homes because their families are separated, with many family members living in different cities or states because this is where they work. And the aging parents now have to go to these elder-care homes where exorbitant prices are charged for their care. In a community that is organized with the love of the elderly in mind, the elderly are cared for when they are old and sick and dying. Many older people in community live longer and are more active and fulfilled because, although they may not have their biological grandchildren with them, they do have many children they can care for and who love them and call them Grandmother and Grandfather.

Society has learned to put not only the elderly in institutions but the young too, who cannot deal with the lack of love in a materialistic, modern society. These often brilliant and talented young people are diagnosed as bi-polar or some other label and given drugs as the answer to their mental malaise. So these young people carry the stigma of some mental illness that psychiatrists have labeled them with, when all they actually need is a community of people loving and watching over them and an eldership guiding and helping them to meet their individual destinies that God has ordained for them.

Many of these dysfunctional teens and young adults come from single-parent families because of divorce, and the one parent does not suffice for two loving parents as well as an extended family.

The idea of a highest destiny for a young person is lost in modern-day society, because the relatives of that youth or child are no longer in the same neighborhood. Not too many relatives can really observe that child on a daily basis and see his or her developing talents, and so the child cannot be guided and given the tools and instruments within that communal care to meet his or her destiny. This is why some troubled young people are killing each other in schools in mass shootings because these individuals (even though they may be living with parents and have relatives) are not really living in a loving communal reality.

Many of these children end up in wrong careers and have to take jobs instead of getting an education for their true vocation or being trained in a career because there is no real elder guiding them in the right direction. So they end up taking jobs in labor, retail stores, factories, law enforcement, and the postal service or join the military whenever they are of age, because they cannot afford a quality guitar to become a musician or paint and brushes to become an artist or any kind of education to become what is in their hearts to become. So their dreams are lost very early in life, and many of their parents push them to earn a living rather than follow their hearts. Some musicians do not get a quality guitar until they are in their thirties or forties and by then they are really too old to do much in their career. This is not true of everyone, but there are thousands of individuals who simply do not have the money to buy the training or the tools and equipment they need to make their dreams come true.

On the other side of the coin, many musicians—like Kurt Cobain, Amy Winehouse, even Whitney Houston—die very young and even commit suicide, because they lost their way due to having no eldership or having a lost sense of family connection to guide them into their proper use of talents. When you sing or write a song that teaches something to help a person grow, these are usually your gifts for God and for humanity—not just singing a romantic song about a lost love or a new love. Without the purpose of educating or uplifting others with your talents, your talents have no real purpose. And many of these artists who become famous find that out all too late.

Many of these artists, who realize they have talent, think they have to go off to Hollywood or New York, cut a record, become famous, make millions, and that is the way to success. But true success is the relationships that you live everyday within a communal family who loves you and you love them. So modern television shows, like *Entertainment Tonight* and *Insider* that propagate stardom, are shows that feed poison to the minds of the young people who watch them.

Modern magazines that are flashy, sexual, and supposedly hip have taken the place of true art and literature. Magazines, television, the computer social network, and even radio have taken the place of family gatherings and community gatherings where people just converse with each other face-to-face, sharing how the day went, sharing talents, and maybe even cooking some special dessert or bread for everybody. So the art of communal interrelationships has been lost to modern media in all its forms of propaganda, selling Western civilization on the latest movie star, sports hero, clothes, makeup, and all the things they say you need to be happy—when all you need to really be happy is be surrounded by loving family and friends.

Modern amusement parks—with all their rides, games of chance, haunted houses, and live entertainment—have taken the place of communal activities such as hiking in nature, boating, fishing, and horse riding. Instead of just jumping on a horse in an amusement park and going around in a circle, adopt a horse and get to know it by everyday helping to feed and brush it. You will find out that the horse has a "horse-onality" too and loves the human attention. Amusement parks were built for people who live in cities in urban realities.

The problem with most urban realities is they really are inhumane realities. And today's cities, with millions of people, are cities of distortion and delusional energies. (See *The Cosmic Family, Volume I*, Paper 215 for more information on these energies that cause erratic and disturbed behavior.) In order for society today to come back to sanity, people need to come back to the land, to the earth, to rural and communal living.

People need to come out of living in toxic boxes, because most of the housing built is not built with non-toxic materials in mind. They contain chemicals in the paint, and the plaster, and the carpets, and people die of cancers because of these chemicals and toxins. The cities can temporarily still be places where people work but should not be where they live permanently. They should try to make their living within the community income businesses that serve the world at large, and in this manner they do not even have to drive to work.

People are not made by God to live crammed in crowded high-rises, apartment buildings, and so on. They are not meant to live surrounded by cement and asphalt. They are meant to live in natural settings because in nature is the essence of the Universe Mother Spirit. And people need to experience Her spirit everyday—not just once a week or once month when you maybe get away from the city, but on an everyday basis, interacting with the grass, hugging a tree, going in the creek, or putting your feet in a pond and watching the ducks play in it. Basically human beings become crazed in some way in city life. They become despondent, angry, lonely, feeling inadequate, and often overeat to try to replace that emptiness that they feel from urban life.

The world seems to be getting more inhospitable. There is unrest all over the world because people have lost touch with each other, and leaders have lost touch with the people. This is a breeding ground for rebellion, anarchy, and war.

I am calling for people to move to the country, live in a communal situation with individuals, grow your own food, have a good water source, build green, and have as many things in common as possible with your extended communal family. If the economic crisis gets worse, you may find you may not have any choice but to do this, and by then (if you wait too long), it may be too late for the survival of yourself, your children, and grandchildren.

PART 3

The Loneliness, Stress, Isolation, And Lack Of Human Compassion And Support Of Brothers And Sisters Existing In Urban Life. The Need For Community And Coming Back To Nature

We should ask ourselves how many people should comfortably live in close proximity to one another, also in relationship to working and using the same recreation facilities. For instance, New York City has an approximate ten-mile radius (which includes the boroughs) with roughly twenty million inhabitants within that radius. In our extra-large cities of more than ten million people, how big should that radius be?

The answer to that is really difficult to figure out today because cities have suburbs and smaller towns surrounding it that create one continual urban area. Los Angeles, for example, extends north and south, so everywhere in southern California is crowded. You might say that all of southern California and north to Malibu is one big city.

Most eastern cities are the same way—Chicago, Washington, D.C., Philadelphia, Boston, Pittsburgh, and many more—all extending well beyond the specified city boundaries, and you have to drive at least 50–100 miles from downtown to get out to any rural areas. When people on city sidewalks look like ants in an ant colony—bumping into each other and crawling over each other—shouldn't you begin to realize something is wrong? When traffic jams are backed up for miles and miles, and sometimes for hours at a time, shouldn't you begin to ask if this kind of lifestyle is healthy for you or your family? Is it worth the money you are making?

Stress is one of the major reasons that people die of various heart problems, loss of vital organs, and other major medical situations. It is not just the stress from work-related problems that kills you. It is living and working in an environment where stress cannot be alleviated properly. For example, working in an overcrowded office in a high-rise, or even if you are working in a high-rise in your own private luxury office, it is still a high-rise, and the pollution rises right up to meet your stress. So do not open a window!

And when you go down to the first floor and go outside and walk out on the street, do not inhale there either, because it is not clean air you are breathing, it is the toxins from thousands of automobiles and other industrial pollutants in the air that kill you just as invisibly but yet as literally as someone coming up to you and putting a gun to your head and pulling the trigger.

People are told by the American Medical Association that they are living longer today. Most people today, even if they live to be in their sixties, seventies, eighties and even nineties, actually have tired and unhealthy bodies, and often the poor health begins in their forties and early fifties.

I am amazed to hear sports broadcasters referring to boxers and other athletes as being "over the hill" when in their thirties. I think that much of their fast aging is because these athletes are living in urban areas, not so much because the sport is doing it to them. Those athletes who do not live in urban areas are usually healthier. Those boxers and other athletes who train in urban areas should find that their energy levels are lower than those who train in rural areas who can last into the later rounds with more energy and power.

Everything in urban life is meant to stimulate the senses and mind but not the soul. It is the soul that actually houses the mind, and the physical body temporarily houses the soul. When the physical body begins to break down, the soul will suffer too, unless one feeds the soul the way it is supposed to be fed: with nature, clean water, organic food, the camaraderie of living with significant others, and of course treating other people kindly and taking time for them, which is something that city life does not promote in its "hurry up" atmosphere.

In a large city people often are lonely, even though the population of the city they are living in can be millions of people. However it is not just living in smaller cities that leads to prolonged life and better health and healthier aging. It is living in true community, where a communal aspect of life feeds the soul—that is having as many material things in common with others as possible and sharing those things, sharing living spaces while having adequate privacy (as opposed to two people living in a 6,000 or 7,000 sq. ft. home), sharing automobiles, and passing clothing down to others. Most of all, instead of living in overcrowded urban neighborhoods (even if you live in a cul-de-sac and think that is more privacy), true community is the joining with five, ten, twenty, or thirty people to buy some land in the countryside with adequate acreage for the number of people, where you can see some open spaces and trees and horses, instead of stray dogs and cats, and (unfortunately for many poor in this country) living with rats.

Perhaps you may say to yourself now, "Where can I find these other people to put my limited finances with to buy land in rural America?" Perhaps you may not have any finances at all, but you have talents to offer that contribute to building the infrastructure of the community and maintaining its upkeep. Perhaps you have computer skills, or gardening experience, or cooking abilities, or a knack for caring for children. Whatever it is that is practical, those are valuable assets.

You are never going to find those people to build community with unless you take the steps to find them. It may be as simple as talking to strangers, going to coffee houses, putting ads in the paper if you can, making flyers, using bulletin boards, even looking to see what communities have already been formed that you can join. The Internet is a good source. There is also a magazine called *Communities* that lists intentional communities across the United States.

With the onslaught of modern civilization and industrialization, the once-tribal communities—that understood the value of living and working and playing with other human beings, called neighbors—are no longer part of living, real living. Now people move to cities to find work. But what good is work and making money if it takes up all your time getting to and from the job and then when you come home you are too tired to interact with your family? And you do the same thing every day and long for the weekend that is no longer really restful. Unless you get out into the rural areas, that weekend is usually a loss too for finding reprieve from stress. That is why most people try to get away on the weekends. Instinctually people know they want to go somewhere where they can breathe more deeply and slowly, be near water or in the mountains or in the open spaces, smelling the flowers (instead of the garbage).

You would be surprised how much money you do not need once you live in true community life and what ten, twenty, thirty, forty, or fifty committed people can accomplish when working together for a common purpose. You can live in beautiful environments that you would never be able to afford if you would try to buy that kind of living environment on your own.

Urban life and being independent of others is the kind of thinking that has caused the isolation and loneliness of people in Western civilization. People have become more selfish, and the idea of being your brother's and sister's keeper does not even come into the modern mind. You should be able to help raise the children of other extended families in real practical ways and be a part of those children's raising, not just your own children of your immediate family.

This can be done in a communal living situation where it cannot be done in the isolation of box houses in a suburban neighborhood where you hardly ever see your neighbors or their children and you may think you should have nothing to do with the raising of these children. There is an ancient saying, "It takes a whole tribe to raise a child."

Living with animals is the way of nature between animals and humans. This too has been lost in urban life. In the cities, animals are kept in cages called zoos. (Actually the zoos are where some people should be living, for they are the real "animals" when it comes to consciousness.) People in urban life may get their children a dog or a cat, but in rural life, living on a farm, they can also play with chickens, goats, cattle, pigs, emus, rabbits, and horses. Children come to know more about these animals when they live near them on the same land.

Many of these children do decide to become vegetarians because they grew up with these animals and know that they have a life too, that they have babies and care for their young. To urban children, the chicken or beef or pork are bought at the local supermarket without any consciousness that they were once living and breathing creatures of God. I am not saying that everyone should be a vegetarian, although I do think that a higher consciousness of animal life is needed by meat eaters, particularly those who eat beef, pork, and chicken.

People live and die in cities and have never really been to a farm to see how these animals live.

When you do, you begin to find out that these animals need space and to be cared for. So too do humans need space and to be cared for, and most cities do not really provide for the spiritual, physical, and emotional needs of human beings today. This is one of the reasons why there is so much mental illness happening on the planet today. This is one of the reasons why young teenagers are killing each other, as well as adults flipping out in city life, because the energies there are distorted and dysfunctional.

Unfortunately there are people who do not want community and move to the country, build the same kind of toxic homes, live in close proximity to each other but have no neighborly contact, and in time another suburban environment develops in the once-pristine countryside.

Unfortunately there are contractors who even claim to "build green," when the only thing green about their building projects is the paint on the walls. Developers take a pristine country setting and build condos or timeshares, and people buy them as second homes. And many of these large developments, with hundreds of clone-like homes, have names that imply peaceful, country living that is not the case at all; they are extensions of the city.

There is no substitute for true country living and true community life, no matter how you try to market the decoy. I recently passed through a golf resort area (another tragedy of modern times) with a development that was called "The Mission." They had other names, for streets, like "Chapel Way,"

"Meditation Way"—you get the idea. It sounded so good that Jesus Himself would buy a condo!

Many counties in the United States need to have stronger laws against these kinds of irresponsible and non-sustainable developments, particularly counties in the rural areas that are still left, or these counties will become one big city instead of a rural county with open space, and the countrysides across America will be lost to greedy developers and unconscious buyers of these modern toxic homes and anti-community developments.

A Series Of 3 Articles In Relationship To The Deterioration Of The Earth And All Its Systems— Climatic, Resources, Food, Economic, And Consciousness

PART 1

The Occupy Movement Needs To Fuse With The Spiritualution℠ Movement To Win Against The 1%

I do not think that the Mayans or the ancient Egyptians or Nostradamus or the Hopi or other indigenous peoples or any one spiritual ideology has all the answers pertaining to how the Creator works with humans to accomplish the fight against evil. We can only find these answers at a beginning level in the Continuing Fifth Epochal Revelation that explains the physics of rebellion, published in *The Cosmic Family* volumes, a work that is unknown to almost all of the billions of people on this planet.

Many people (particularly in the United States) think that anything spiritual has to do with someone getting in your face trying to "save" you, because Christian fundamentalists and evangelicals (who are basically one and the same) have scared most people with common sense away from any spiritual approach to the Creator. Even "Jesus Christ" has become two dirty words in America. Most people think that becoming spiritual means going to church on Sundays, or to synagogue on Saturdays, or worshiping in Moslem mosques or Hindu temples.

That is going to a place of worship rather than going inside one's self.

If one really studies history, he or she can come to a conclusion that some people, who do really have some relationship with the Creator, seem to reach positions of influence, and those particular persons make a difference in this world by creating renaissances of higher spiritual, social, and political consciousness throughout history. Against all odds, these spiritually-minded people overcome great obstacles to accomplish that which seems impossible.

So too does the present Occupy movement need this kind of assistance from the Creator. No movement that is righteous can win unless the people within the movement have varying degrees of righteousness within themselves. That does not mean that these people are religious fanatics, fundamentalists, legalists, or church goers. It does however mean, as Gandhi said, the individual first has to "be the change" for the movement to really be effective. Gandhi took on the military power of the British Empire by nonviolent resistance and civil disobedience and won! At one point he fasted, almost to death, until the people of all India stopped any anarchism and violence that occurred.

To have the power to change circumstantial reality from evil to good, one must overcome the evil that you want to change in others—be it individuals or systems or corporations. Without adopting the virtues of the Creator within one's self, you cannot change the corporate executives, the politicians, the police, or any evil person in any position of power.

Jesus gave the commands as to how to defeat the enemy when He said that you need to put on the full armor of God: the helmet of salvation (being in relationship with the Creator), the breastplate of righteousness (being a kind person, so that you do not receive an unkind thought or deed back to you), the sword of the Spirit (letting your words mean what they say and say what they mean, and not speaking with a forked tongue), the shoes of peace (walking in harmony and unity with all people of all religions), the shield of faith (knowing that a higher power is with you when you have right motive), and creating a righteous standard for yourself (walking the walk, not just talking the talk—if you do not do it, do not expect the 1% to do it).

Just as there are civil laws and ordinances, and consequences for anyone who disobeys these laws, in the spiritual realm it works like that too, even more so. As one matures on this fallen world (which one can also call the third dimension), one must raise one's consciousness to understand these spiritual principles of karma or cause and effect.

The Continuing Fifth Epochal Revelation presents the two concepts of ascension science and the physics of rebellion (as well as many others) that are revelatory. The Occupiers call their movement a rebellion, but they need to take this rebellion up a notch, because it has to be a rebellion inside themselves, against every form of evil within themselves—not just a rebellion against the evil 1%-ers.

The Family Concept

The Continuing Fifth Epochal Revelation is presented in *The Cosmic Family* volumes—"cosmic family" because the idea of family is the highest ideal that one understands as the most important thing in life. And individuals must find a family (if their family of birth is dysfunctional) at some point in their sojourn on the earth or they will be disoriented, dysfunctional, and basically either outcasts from society or fall into the criminal element.

The Occupy movement needs to be more of a family. Families have elders—grandparents, parents, older brothers, older sisters, aunts, uncles, cousins. In the extended family they all protect each other. Those families throughout history who have had the greatest virtues within themselves (like love, joy, peace, patience, kindness, non-competitiveness, non-jealous tendencies, and protection of each other) have been the most successful families, even in the financial realms, as their corporative ventures were not set up for greed but for serving humanity. They were "corporations of love" not corporations of profit. The Jews and the Mormons are a couple of examples of groups who have been successful in their financial endeavors because of their group or family love and looking out for one another.

These hierarchies of family love overcame many obstacles that came against their businesses of serving others (when the 1% throughout history tried to destroy them) by the families' respect for their elders and adhering to their counsel. In the onslaught of the industrial age, the 1% began to breakdown the family, the eldership, the hierarchies of love, the corporations of love, and replace them with the corporations of profit.

Before the industrial age, tribes that were more prosperous with growing food, hunting and gathering, or anything that had to do with surviving as a family unit, were actually attacked by the military and legions of the 1%. The Roman legions were an example of the power of the 1% Senate and Caesars who ruled without the concept of love and service to humanity.

Around 30–45 A.D. the Roman legions and their best generals found the most difficult armies and leaders they had to face in the ancient Isle of Avalon in Britain, because these were fierce fighters protecting what they valued and loved. These were the tribes of the Silures, the Celts, the Picts, and others. These more family-oriented tribes had adopted at a beginning level the understanding of one Creator for all humankind and believed in an afterlife, which gave them a sense of what is of eternal value. They were the first to adopt the new teachings of The Way, the teachings of Jesus Christ before they were distorted. Jesus Christ did not teach much of what has become modern Christianity. He taught the Fatherhood of God and the brother-/sisterhood of all humankind. And though Jesus Christ did not teach war tactics or using military force, in their struggle for survival and defense against invaders who were motivated by lust for power and greed, these tribes were more unified due to their greater love for each other and a stronger sense of protectiveness.

Every renaissance movement throughout history had a spiritual concept behind it. It was a Spiritualution movement, a spiritual revolution—people seeking justice for religious and social freedom. The majority of the people knew that without the help of the Creator they would not win against the 1% of their day and the 1%'s military and financial might.

The Occupy movement today needs also to discover "The Way." People all over the world need to discover "The Way." And this "Way" does not have to do with religions; it has to do with family. It has to do with community. It has to do with sharing. It has to do with having all things in common. It has to do with giving rather than getting. It has to do with putting the other person before yourself. It has to do with helping other people in any way you can, to help them meet their destinies, by supplying (if you can) what they need, the tools they may need, the instruments they may need, the materials they may need. It has to do with all citizens of the earth seeing themselves as part of "One God, One Planetary Family."

This is the way to defeat the 1%'s greedy grabbing. Demonstrations alone will not do it, even though civil disobedience is much better than any form of violence or force or take over by coup. Many a people of many a land have discovered that when new forms of government replace evil forms of government, those new forms of government become corrupted themselves over time, if there is not an inner change in the populace who elects the officials or in the officials themselves.

The people's movement should be a movement of families and corporate love. A people's movement can only be successful if the people want change for the benefit of the other person, not for themselves. When the movement is for themselves, the people's revolutions have failed. So if you have 10,000 demonstrators saying "We are the people" and the majority of them are actually angry because "things are not happening for them," even if change happens to some degree, it will not last, because there has to be a majority of those demonstrators who are demonstrating for the common good of all. Oh, they may say they are, but history has proven otherwise, even in America (with all of our so-called "freedoms") that is fast becoming a fascist state.

As long as racism exists in America or the world, as long as greed, jealousy, resentment, and the quest for dio (evil) power exists, not much will really change. You cannot depend upon just one or a few leaders to have godly virtues, for they too will pass on, and new leaders will have to be appointed. If there are not many Godly leaders among the citizens, then others less Godly will probably be elected and appointed. The more Godly leaders you have among the people, the longer justice will prevail.

Good and honorable bills have been thrown out of Congress and the Senate here in America because the majority of the Congress and the Senate are not really Godly men and women. If they were, these bills would pass. One recently was the 1% paying at least an equal percentage of taxes as the 99% do.

Our country has lost its "Way" because the masses have been bombarded by the evil of the corporate media in television, movies, music, and magazines. Sex, violence, the desire for stardom, profit, and greed have become the gods of the people of America and have spread their evil influence over most of the world.

When the majority of Americans for the last 235 years kept to "The Way" and family, they had the corporate love power. The people ruled, not the 1%. Over the last fifty or more years, gradually the 99% have given over the power to the 1% because the 99% have bought the propaganda of the 1%.

Today there are more students of physics and spirituality who know how these two seemingly contradicting subjects fuse together to affect reality as we know it in the physical, mindal, and spiritual world. And many progressive physics students know that the mind seems to affect particles when looking through a microscope. This is called the Heisenberg Principle. Therefore we get the equation "energy follows thought."

All of these concepts that I am giving may seem to be too hard to grasp. That is because the 1% wants to keep you in lower consciousness. That is why they bombard you with the garbage you see and hear in various media forms. They do not want you to discover epochal revelation—*The URANTIA Book* and the Continuing Fifth Epochal Revelation (*The Cosmic Family* volumes). The 1% and those who follow their direction have tried to reduce *The URANTIA Book* to an extraterrestrial book of metaphysical nonsense.

They have done their best to also discredit my work in *The Cosmic Family* volumes, misrepresent my character, and use whatever they can to do this, particularly apostates from "The Way." So you do not find these books very popular, or my music on the radio, or see me on television. And you will not see or hear any leader who is really walking and teaching "The Way" on the mainstream media that is owned and controlled by the 1%.

But what they do not know is that this is the dawn of a new age. The first stage of light and life on Urantia (Earth) is coming. The Rebellion has to end on this planet, a rebellion that started 200,000 years ago by a celestial being called Caligastia (who was on this earth as its Planetary Prince), who followed the lies of another celestial being called Lucifer. Both of these characters Christianity calls "The Devil" or "Satan." What is happening now on this planet is the culmination of this Rebellion. This culmination is called the adjudication of the Bright and Morning Star versus Lucifer.

The Rehabilitation Of Outer Space In The System Of Satania Is Happening Too

Outer space itself is reacting to this upstepping of the end of the Rebellion, for the closer the Promised One—also known as Lord Maitreya by the Buddhists, Imam Mahdi by the Moslems, Kalki Avatar by the Hindus, The Messiah by the Jews, or

Jesus Christ by Christians (to name a few)—comes to the earth (in a mighty awesome architectural world), the particles themselves in the atmosphere above the earth and in our solar system react, as many scientists today are discovering but do not know why.

A Russian scientist by the name of Alexey Demetriev has many articles about the cosmic changes that are occurring in space, which is this phenomenon I referred to in the previous paragraph. *The Cosmic Family* volumes teach, in relationship to celestial mechanics, that the closest six inhabited planets to or in the administrative system of Satania that have already settled in the stages of light and life are aligning with Urantia/Earth. This alignment is already causing cosmic events that contribute to the earthquakes, volcanic eruptions, climate change, and so on.

You might say that the Promised One is coming to Occupy Earth.

PART 2

The Invisible War

For those in the Occupy movement or any activist who is trying to make change within the existing "system" about anything, they can no longer ignore what is happening to global civilization and the planet as a whole—financially, socially, politically, environmentally, spiritually, etc. They cannot ignore any longer the spiritual aspect or the Spiritualution℠ movement that is taking place all over the earth, even if millions of people who are crying out for change are unaware that they are part of this movement.

They can no longer ignore the prophecies of the Old Testament and Book of Revelation in the Bible, nor the predictions of Nostradamus, the Hopi, the Mayans, and other indigenous cultures where their holy men have prophesized about these times, which the Occupy movement all over the world is fulfilling on the level of helping to change people's consciousness.

In his book *The Crisis Of Civilization And How To Save It*, the author Nofeez Mosaddeq Ahmed lists these seven points of what is happening to the earth:

1. climate change
2. peak oil
3. food shortage
4. economic crisis
5. the threat of international terrorism

6. militarization
7. the post-peak-oil world

I would like to elaborate on these seven points from a spiritual perspective, bringing about a Spiritualution consciousness, rather than from just the physical perspective of the author in his book (although he is very in touch with what will happen if these issues are not addressed by the majority of people on this planet very quickly).

1. Climate Change

As written in my books, *The Cosmic Family* volumes, negative thoughts affect the particles in the atmosphere, the clouds, the air we breathe, the water, the soil—everything. It is not just cleaning up the environment that Ahmed points out we need to do; it is cleaning up our minds that we mostly need to do, because even if we could clean up all of the pollution, toxic waste, and all of the other physical problems in the environment that we humans have caused by our greed, the world would still self-destruct because of the negative mindset we have toward each other, for one reason or another—be it religion, politics, or just plain jealousies.

In previous articles, I have mentioned the alignment of six other inhabited planets that are closest to earth that have settled in light and life and are now aligning with the earth, which is expanded upon in *The Cosmic Family* volumes. As I pointed out in Part 1 of this series of articles, these energies are powerful and are just beginning to be discovered in outer space by scientists, though they do not know exactly what these space energies and activities are. But no device on Earth can measure the kinds of changes that will happen as these six other planets come more into alignment with the earth.

Global warming will accelerate, and the meltdown of glaciers will happen at an alarming and destructive rate to a "suddenly" point when all ice will melt everywhere simultaneously. This will of course lead to mass flooding of our coastlines, up to hundreds of miles inland. Other drastic earth changes will happen, which I will elaborate on in future articles. But the main thing is that due to these catastrophic events, human beings will respond by becoming more good or more evil, and this will be increasingly noticeable by anyone with any kind of discernment.

2. Peak Oil

There is plenty of oil under the earth, but the problem is the use of it, as it is not the kind of energy that humankind really should be using any longer. Actually if the Lucifer Rebellion had not occurred (200,000 years ago), higher forms of energy would have been discovered on this planet. But greed and hunger for power have dominated the 1% who have ruled economics, politics, and governments throughout all of the ages, and this has prevented humankind's spiritual and consciousness growth in technical advancements, because all three—spirituality, economics, and politics—relate to each other (although some would argue with this point).

The 1% worldwide would be willing to keep oil as the main source of energy and keep control of the oil and rake in the profits forever, regardless of the destructive impact on the earth and its peoples. And they do this by keeping education in the hands of their own families and keeping the poor from being educated in higher schools of learning and thought. At least the 1% think they do, but the truth is they cannot keep spiritual truth away from the seeker of "The Way." Poor people may not be able to attend Harvard, but that is OK, because in this present world Harvard teaches how to establish more oil fields and the business of marketing oil and all of its products. From lipstick to deodorants to plastic, just about everything has petroleum by-products in it. Harvard and other universities may have schools of theology, but wisdom comes only from God; you cannot pay any price to buy it.

You would be surprised what the true seeker of "The Way" will be given by the Creator, both physically and mentally, to accomplish great things for humanity and even become financially prosperous, as long as that seeker is trying to serve humankind and not himself or herself.

The seekers will bring about new inventions, but the entitlement to making those inventions available to the world and profiting financially from them usually belongs to the 1%. People serving themselves will learn how to keep the 1% rich, and very few of those in the 99% who do get degrees today can even pay off their loans, let alone become part of the 1% (like they are promised).

3. Food Shortage

Before humankind divided the earth by surveys, fences, and borders, there was plenty of food grown all over the earth, and much of it without even farming it. It just happened naturally—fruit trees and vegetables of all kinds (some of which have gone extinct, and the seeds have been long lost). There is enough good agricultural land on this planet to feed many more people. The problem is not really overpopulation (though that will soon be the case); the problem is greed and control by the 1%, which uses agricultural practices that deplete the nutritional value of the soil and of the food being grown. Now it is speculated that even chemtrails are dropped over us to destroy all natural organic food crops and seeds, because those in control of food production want us to become dependent and slaves to genetically-engineered vegetables, fruits, and grains.

I do not want to elaborate on what you can read about from other sources concerning the destruction of food and lack of sustainability and ecosystems and the need for permaculture. Although we at Avalon Organic Gardens & EcoVillage practice principles of sustainable living and organic farming, very few people practice "spiritual organics" and another term that I came up with several years ago, "soulistic healing."

Plenty of people who eat organically become vegans and raw foodists and still discover that they too become sick and diseased with something. So what is the cause of their "dis-eases"? Could it be that their dis-eases are a result of wrong thinking, of evil in their minds? As much as the 1% try everything they can do to live longer lives, they will find out that they will die just like everybody else, and many of them a lot faster than the poorest person in the ghetto or the indigenous people in the mountains.

The body indeed is a temple of the Creator, and *The URANTIA Book* teaches that a Thought Adjuster (of the Universal Father) works with the mind, as does the Spirit of Truth (from the Eternal Son), and the Holy Spirit (of the Universe Mother Spirit). All three can be activated by one's freewill choice to become a seeker of "The Way."

Peter the Apostle was put in prison in Rome, tied to a post, and kept there for nine months in a dark, dingy, smelly, disgusting environment and given only a little water and scraps to eat, but he survived, because during his imprisonment he led hundreds of other followers of "The Way" to a higher faith in the Universal Father to be able to face the lions in the arena. I guarantee you that none of the 1% who control the man-made systems of this world could survive those Roman prisons and those same circumstances for too long.

The point that I am trying to make is that although people die of starvation on this planet, they ascend automatically to a much better world. And those who are guilty of keeping them in poverty are actually dying to eternity with every thought of greed that comes into their mind.

The First Garden in Dalamatia (the headquarters of the Planetary Prince, which some in the New Age call Atlantis) with Van and Amadon (see *The URANTIA Book*) was meant to eventually feed the whole world, as was the second Garden of Eden, with Adam and Eve, meant to do the same. There will come a Third Garden of Eden that will fulfill the purpose of feeding the world, and many of the 99% who wish to be part of this great humanitarian endeavor will be part of a council called The Council of Food and Material Welfare.

4. Economic Crisis

Since money, and not barter or trade, has been the means of obtaining what you need for survival (besides farming, hunting, and gathering), the wants of humankind—not the needs—have been the desire of the hearts of greed. Wall Street in some manner has always been with us. It is that wall between the rich and the poor, the haves and the have-nots, the educated and the uneducated. Nothing really has changed, just new players in the control of a few over the majority.

Capitalism, as we know and experience it in materialistic America, will eventually come to an end, and there is a spiritual reason behind this too. If the principles of the Creator are not being upheld— for instance, being your brother's and sister's keeper, doing unto others as you would have them do unto you—the laws of cause and effect put in place by the Creator will bring an end to the consciousness of greed and selfishness.

It is inevitable that a Divine New Order has to take place over the old order of all the money in the hands of a few, basically 1% of the world. A new system of sharing natural resources, created resources, and talents will be the modus operandi of that Divine New Order.

5. International Terrorism

In actuality, the 1% promote fear in the populace worldwide so that you would look to their military and police state as your protectors against the "terrorists." Most of these so-called terrorists are actually freedom fighters against the oppression of the 1% (not that there aren't actually terrorists on all sides who are not honorable soldiers protecting the innocent, but madmen who murder indiscriminately innocent men, women, and children).

Included as the real terrorists are the 1% whose mercenaries fly over the indigenous in their helicopters and machine gun down innocent civilians to take their resources—be it oil, trees, minerals, whatever. They bomb innocent men, women, and children, even using the term "collateral damage" to obtain their lands. The term "terrorism" is used by the imperialists to control all of us.

The 1% takes away the freedoms of Americans by passing laws to protect us—supposedly from the terrorists—and keep us in fear of a made-up enemy that the 1% has created by their propaganda and imperialistic tactics. These laws have names like The Patriot Act and the National Defense Authorization Act.

In the United Kingdom, in 2004, the Civil Contingencies Act was passed that can arrest any citizen for just about anything. Former Minnesota Governor Jesse Ventura said when a government starts telling you they want to protect you more, be careful, they are about to take your freedoms away. Calling an unknown enemy "terrorists" keeps the 1%'s war going in the minds and hearts of the fearful Americans and Europeans. (I am not denying that there are acts of terrorism—killing of the innocent—going on in many countries, and terrorism is certainly a reality, but you must be careful to not be unrealistically fearful of terrorism happening to you and thus controlled by the fear tactics of the 1%.)

6. Militarization

Jesus said that one day the meek will inherit the earth. But for now for the last 200,000 years since the Lucifer Rebellion and the fall of Caligastia (the fallen Planetary Prince of Earth who accepted the lies and tenets of Lucifer, the fallen System Sovereign), men on Earth have had to have a club to protect themselves or their families from others who wanted what they had. And those with the biggest clubs were the ones who took what they wanted.

Weaponry has advanced, and those with the most powerful weapons and means to employ them rule the world. The 1% in civilization, beginning with the Caesars of Rome and Emperors like them, B.C. and A.D., controlled the world of their time. When greed and selfishness rule, "might is right."

But it is written in scriptures, "Not by power nor by might but by the Spirit, sayeth the Lord."

The military supposedly keeps the peace, but the truth is, it often just creates more wars. The countries with the biggest nuclear stockpiles do not want the other countries to get them, under the guise that "these other countries are dangerous." The truth is that any country with a nuclear weapon is dangerous because the Creator never intended that weapons be the means to bring peace to society.

God does not want humans to choose to follow His truths, principles, laws, statutes, and even commandments due to fear of Him. He wants human beings to follow His laws and principles based on divine love because it is the right thing to do and because it is the choice of love that serves others rather than serving one's self. The lesson to choose to put another before one's self finally has to be learned, once and for all, for all humanity. And when this lesson is finally learned by every soul, then true peace will come to the earth and the lion will lie with the lamb.

7. The Post-Peak-Oil World

Only through a worldwide Spiritualution movement will the world survive without complete and total deterioration and destruction of the earth. The world systems that are based on selfishness and greed are failing. Only by being your brother's and sister's keeper (as is spoken about in the very first book of the Old Testament, Genesis) will the world be able to survive without the Promised One returning and setting up an immediate planetary Divine Administration.

There has to be a redefinition of civilization and what true civilization really is. Civility does not equal spirituality. Evil men can appear to be civil. It all looks good on the outside, but behind closed doors another evil reality is perpetrated by the civil hypocrites. People must unselfishly meet other people's needs, and by doing that their own needs will be met.

The concept of family has to become prominent again in the hearts of all peoples everywhere, a concept that includes eldership and respect for that eldership's authority—the grandfathers, the grandmothers. We must understand soul age and the reality of cosmic parents and cosmic grandfathers and grandmothers. Chronological age is not always pertinent to identify an elder. This is why *The Cosmic Family* volumes are so important and vital in understanding the future administration of planetary government.

Community has to take the place of individual materialism. A true communal lifestyle has to become the norm, and the 1% cannot own or control the land, because all people everywhere have to have access to land to grow their own crops and have natural resources. Free education and healthcare have to be available to every man, woman, and child all over this earth.

Only in this manner will new and innovative inventions be thought of and built by minds previously held in the bondage of poverty and slavery and serfdom. Celebrity status has to completely be a thing of the past. People must see each other as special—not just the people in movies and television—and that people do not have to be on television or the movies to be considered special or talented, and that the greatest and some of the most valuable people will not be the movie stars or rock stars but teachers and true healers, who can use natural substances from the earth rather than synthetic drugs. True spiritual men and women who teach spiritual principles to promote healthy minds, souls, and bodies need to be held in high esteem rather than actors, comedians, talk-show hosts, sports heroes, and so on.

A continuing redefinition of the significance of people's various roles in society must now be in the forefront of the majority of people's minds in the civilized world, or the 1% will continue to promote the idea of being rich and wealthy as the role models, even though they themselves will not let many into their elitist families. Their propaganda is just that. It is meant to make people want what they cannot really have, so that they can keep on trying to get, rather than give—just the opposite of what Jesus taught. To be great in the kingdom of God, He said to give it all away and follow "The Way." He said to be great in the kingdom of God is to be a servant to all.

Look around you. The cost of living, including gasoline and food, is now almost unaffordable for the 99%. Now is the time to start applying these principles that I have mentioned, for when the dio (evil) acceleration of the quantum leap occurs, in all its ugly and horrible destruction of the breaking down of all physical systems of the earth, it will happen very suddenly, when actually it has been going on a downward spiral for decades now. It is too late for the quantum leap of light to happen, and according to the Hopi elders and scientific data, the ecological and man-made (social and economic) systems are quickly deteriorating.

This "suddenly" will be so completely devastating and will happen so quickly that humankind will not know what hit it. Now is the time for all people worldwide to unite, for all people to begin to occupy their own minds and hearts with the Spiritualution principles that I have outlined in this article, while there is still time to lessen the pain and suffering of billions. Let us hope that the times of the purification of the Hopi can be shortened by the further changing of consciousness within a worldwide Spiritualution movement and that the slogan "Spiritualution—Justice To the People" (gesture: fist to heart, fist to sky) be the international greeting of the 99%.

PART 3

The "Occupy Movement" Is Actually The Right Name Because The "99%" Is A Misnomer. The Leftover Middle Class Are The Silent Apathy-ites.

The "99%" is correct conceptually but wrong in reality, because there is still a great number of middle class left over from the good ol' days, with enough money in the bank for them to feel secure. As a matter of fact, they do not see themselves as part of the 99%. In this article, I will refer to these "couch sitters" as the apathy-ites. They think the people out on the streets are leftover hippies or the poor who do not want to work or young people who are just looking to cause trouble—even if some of those demonstrators are their own children, who are in debt thousands or tens of thousands of dollars in student loans, with little hope of getting a job in the career they got (or are getting) a degree in.

These parents—baby boomers in the millions—grew up in a time of prosperity when they were able to buy a home, have a car or two in the garage as well as a boat for the weekends, and take vacations at least once a year. Many still have enough left in the bank to continue to live that kind of lifestyle in their retirement years. They were able to send their children to college, and many of their children, when they graduated, still were able to get jobs in their careers. Unfortunately they also became apathy-ites, better known as yuppies. But some of these once-middle-classers ran out of money and are on the streets in the Occupy movement in every city in the United States and all over the world.

However, there is still a great portion of Americans who have not felt the recession enough to get them out of their comfort zones or even to voice their opinions in support of those who consider themselves the 99%, the "Occupiers." Those comfortable people are actually part of the 99%, but they think (because they are still comfortable) that the system works and that it is OK if the rich are rich (and getting richer) and that they are just comfortable.

What these comfortable couch sitters do not realize is that this type of thinking worked in the 1950s and even '60s, but the opportunities for middle-class living started to slowly deteriorate in the '70s. Now in 2012, depending upon a number of factors (mostly how much money is in their bank accounts), the apathy-ites will be joining the ranks of the poor and will definitely consider themselves as part of the 99%—perhaps sooner than they would think.

Apathy is a terrible thing. Any person who travels to a tourist town to see its special beauty of lakes or rivers or oceans or snow-capped mountains sees a conglomeration of people—tourists as well as gated-community seasonal residents—who are oblivious to the sufferings of the rest of the country and world. We need to start feeling embarrassed about going to these places of smug comfort and apathy while an increasing number of Americans can hardly put food on the table and keep a roof over their children's heads.

The corporate-controlled news sources on television, radio, and other media outlets and their advertising promote the good life. They may show some short clips of the protestors, of the poor, but it is always in the context of "they are the few." For instance, May Day was a day of solidarity for workers, and hundreds of thousands of people demonstrated in the streets of major American cities, but ABC, CBS, NBC, CNN, and definitely Fox gave little attention to any of the people's May Day protests. When any of these news programs did give attention, they downplayed the amount of people in the streets, always showing the few who were anarchists or unruly looking, to make it look like the Occupy movement consists of mostly violent troublemakers.

For the life of me, I could never understand how the commentators (so-called journalists) can report lies and still consider themselves "respectable" news people. How can they face their own children? I guess it is because they have sold out, and the only way we can defeat their propaganda is not to look at their programs. We need to tune in to alternative news networks like Free Speech TV, Link TV, and their programming. We need to demand that the FCC makes other satellite stations for nonprofit media organizations (like the two I mentioned) more available so that there can be many nonprofit media stations with more programs by creative talented artists of all kinds, including innovative producers and musicians who have something to say through their art. Also, unknown speakers need more exposure, because even Free Speech TV and Link TV often act like commercial television and use popular speakers who are too co-operative with government and corporate media. At times these two established alternative sources do not allow speakers and teachers on either station who present an alternative and necessary truth or, if musical, a new genre, and who the stations think would rock the boat too much—be it social, environmental, political, or spiritual truth. They do not present issues that are not en vogue. If they only present what is en vogue, the public will not get an opportunity to hear and see wonderful and new innovative ideas that can help change the world at a faster pace.

There need to be true community radio stations that are not run like regular commercial stations, and the people have to keep an eye on them, because if they are not allowing our voices to be heard on their stations or other music to be played, they are not really a community station. There need to be truly more public television stations. Most of the ones in existence have become too standardized as to who they will put on their programs and what voices they will allow to be heard, based upon who their sponsors are.

Commercial stations are controlled by the profit motive and advertisers. Many community stations, both in radio and television, are controlled by the sponsors giving them big bucks. And before they may play our son's or daughter's music, they will look to see if we are a donor. So we do not want to support these kinds of community radio or television stations. The apathy-ites need to be a lot wiser in who they support today.

The apathy-ites watch "Big Brother" on television, particularly in their retirement years, day and night. And Big Brother is telling them who to vote for (because only the politicians who have sold out can pay for television or radio), what kind of disease they have (and what drugs to take for it), how to dress, what movies they should go to see, and on and on.

This has become the normal way of life for the apathy-ites, but they need to take a good look at the real world, here in America and abroad. What they consider "the real world" has fallen apart for the majority of Americans and people all around the world. Their apathy and turning their eyes away from what is really happening does not really serve their children or grandchildren, or their neighbor's children and grandchildren.

The 1% who feeds these lies to the people of the 99% do not care about them, and when the apathy-ites' money runs out, when their health insurance runs out, they will find out then the hard way—like millions and millions of others have, in America and all over the world—that capitalism works well for the rich and that in the long run the once-middle-class will always become the slaves to the 1%.

Every revolution in history happened because the majority of the people woke up at some point and revolted against their oppressors. When capitalism (control of money in the hands of the few) begins to take the place of precepts of the

Constitution that our Founding Fathers wrote, we become the kind of society that George Orwell wrote about in his book *1984*. We are there. We have been there since 1984, in reality. His timing was close enough. In 1984 in America there were still more comfortable apathy-ites. Now, in 2012, there are many more poor, disenfranchised, and oppressed people who are crying out all over this nation and the world for true freedom.

Freedom in this country was always, for 200 years, true only for the 1% and the middle class, but really never for the poor and disenfranchised, because the 1% and apathy-ites need the majority of people to be controlled so that they can live the good life and keep the poorer people slaves.

So I have to ask those apathy-ites, what is the spirituality you think you have? What is that religion you call yourselves? Because I guarantee you it is not the teachings of Jesus Christ, in this so-called "Christian" country. Jesus never taught Christianity. He taught "The Way," the way of being your brother's and sister's keeper.

His "Way" was for all races and all people all over the world. The 1% like religions because in those religions are the 1% who can keep the people in bondage to their interpretation of the Bible, the Torah, the Vedas, the Book of Mormon, and the Tripitaka and use the pharisaical appointed teachers of these books to be the infallible voices of God—the priests, ministers, rabbis, and imams who actually teach the religions of financial prosperity, fundamentalism, and religious elitism.

It can no longer work for the true holy men and women within these religions who are called by the Creator to serve humanity, because they cannot truly serve humanity in religions that are controlled by the 1%. In reality, it has always been this way. The good and the bad souls have existed side by side in every religion, university, political arena, and work place. But the Rebellion on this planet is coming to a close. Evil is coming to a close.

The good seed is being separated from the bad seed, the wheat from the chaff. The signs are everywhere. If you are blind to these signs, then you too have become too comfortable. Now it is time for true journalists, artists of all kinds, professionals, laborers, and soldiers to walk out of the systems of greed controlled by the 1%, and in particular, the true holy men and women who have been called by the Creator to be ministers in all of the evolutionary religions to come out of them and to walk in "the true Way."

This too goes for the people of all religions to walk out of those religions and systems built by greed and to trust the Creator to provide for you and your family's needs. You have never found out the truth of a true faith walk, because you have been taught by the teachers of the 1% that you need the degrees, their prestigious titles, and badge of success to really succeed in the world. But it is not the world you want to succeed in. It is the kingdom of God that you need to succeed in, for this kingdom is the eternal one. And it begins right here on Earth.

The people of the world need to come together in a radical unity, in a Spiritualution[SM] movement, and unite in this spiritual revolution and help others survive outside of the system of greed and bondage to the 1%. If the 1% has no workers, no slaves, then their dynasties, their banks, their corporations, and their control of natural resources will crumble.

The apathy-ites must understand the words that I have written in this article and begin to see with true spiritual eyes "The Way." They do not have to join a church; I am saying to get out of churches if they are controlled by interests of the rich and filled with other apathy-ites! They do not have to join a religion; I am saying get out of them if they are not of "The Way!" Most religions and the 1%'s control of them have made the words "spirituality" and "God" dirty words. They have made "*The URANTIA Book*" and "*The Cosmic Family* volumes" dirty words, because these books are revelations of "The Way," not teaching religions.

Jesus actually taught the Fatherhood of God and the brotherhood and sisterhood of humankind. Do not throw away Jesus Christ because of modern Christianity. Do not throw away His Father because some people—who do not want to truly practice love, peace, patience, kindness, putting the other person before one's self, and unselfishness—have made these words concepts to avoid. The Father of all sentient, freewill beings on every inhabited world in every universe who have never fallen in a rebellion against their Creator follow "The Way" of the Creator.

It is the 1% who has put God into little boxes and has told humankind: "This is how you have to do it to be a good follower of the Creator." They have used religions as a tool to control the masses. Every person knows that there is right and wrong, good and evil (except for those misguided people who try to make evil good and say that everything is OK). All that God is asking of people is that in the moments of every day they follow their conscience and make decisions for the good of others rather than decisions for selfishness.

Joining the Spiritualution movement worldwide will bring true justice to the people of this world, because it will take the majority of people in the world coming out of the false system and following "The Way" to bring about the quantum leap to bring about the first stage of light and life on Earth, under "One God, One Planetary Family."

True Leaders—
Where Can You Find Them?
How Can You Identify
the False Leaders?
Why Do We Need Leaders?

There is a rift now within the general nationwide Occupy movement between the Declaration (99D) project (who want to set up a New Continental Congress with a new Constitution, mostly organized by a man called Michael Pollok, a New York criminal attorney) and the rest of the Occupy movement, who had a General Assembly meeting in Philadelphia on July 4, 2012, comprised of its many contingencies and organizers from all over the country. It looks as though the 99D group still thinks that change can happen within the existing system, and the Occupy movement organizers believe that real change can only happen outside the current system.

I believe that both sides have correct and incorrect points of view, and the problem is that—as in most differences of opinion—people cannot expand their minds enough to see how another person's or another group's viewpoint may be correct within their own methodology. As I have stated before in many of my published articles, I definitely do not think that real change can happen within the system, and I think that the 99D group is naïve to think that the United States government is going to accept a new Constitution and a new Congress that is not elected by the vast majority of the citizens of this country, mainly because the 1% and its power base of corporate entities and the military will not allow it.

Now these two groups are in division about issues that they should not even try to tackle at this time. In the beginning of the movement, the issue was very clear: stop the control of the 1% over the 99%. Now these two factions are getting sidetracked by arguing whether transgender delegates should be brought in or not. The 99D group seems to discriminate against transgenders while the Occupy movement itself allows for a diversity of thought.

If too much diversity is allowed, then relative thinking that allows for unethical and wrong decisions can occur. And, though diversity is necessary, so is unity of decision and purpose. It seems that balance today is hard to find in any medium, particularly when it involves social and moral issues.

It is all a little confusing at this point, and I think that is because there are so many individuals involved on both sides in consensus decision-making that a clarity of direction cannot be found. Even decisions made in a democracy by majority vote can often elect a policy, an ordinance, a statute, a law, or even a President that is not the overall best for the majority of citizens, the country, or the world.

At this point in humankind's evolution, there have to be regulations on just about everything. If not, for instance, the environment can be (and is already being) destroyed by unethical, profit-motivated industry that pollutes our water, air, and earth; or people get ripped off by financial institutions that charge too high rates for loans and entice faulty investments; or the television and movie industry produces programs and advertising that are not for the highest good of the viewers (especially children) and causes increased malcontent, apathy, selfishness, unease in the mind, and immorality. In a truly civilized society regulations are necessary until most in the society have evolved into being more altruistic and socially responsible citizens.

Though necessary in a truly democratic society, free speech also should have its limitations. For example, when someone advocates anarchism that would destroy all civilizing and regulating influences of an orderly society, this cannot be allowed. When a new culture is being built from the grassroots, disagreement usually occurs as people work out ideas and plans, but continued open dissension can destroy that beginning community, so there have to be more regulations that ensure civil and progressive discussion.

As a community grows to become hundreds of people, then thousands, then hundreds of thousands, then millions, the core government that holds the new culture together can give more opportunity for the people to voice opinions, no matter how openly destructive they may be. Thus here in America—with more than 300 million people in a country that has existed for more than 235 years now—unless someone is advocating violence, they should be allowed to speak. The public will either listen or walk away.

Many people think that when they vote, they are voting for something or someone for the common good of all, but in actuality they are voting for who or what they think is best for them. As I have been saying throughout this book, it does take people with a spiritualized mind and an understanding of what the Spiritualution℠ movement is to bring about true peace and justice for all the people, not only of this country but the world.

Leaders are definitely needed at various positions in government and for a people's republic to function. However, these leaders should not be elected because they agree with your politics. It is politics that have screwed the world up for centuries. Ministers of State should not be elected because they have degrees from Harvard in political science, law, social welfare, or any other degree, or even a degree in theology from Harvard, because these individuals are most likely brand new souls who do not have a multi-dimensional astral past-life experiential mind or soul. They are one-dimensional in how they view many things. That is why they were able to get their degrees. They just answered their tests according to what their teachers wanted. Older souls question everything and usually do not get along with their teachers or professors or the education system, per se.

Throughout modern history, usually newer souls have been the ones elected because most of the people on this planet who vote are new souls too. And the ones running for office are saying what they, the people/new souls, presume to be the truth. The problem is—and it is a big one on this planet—

that a new soul can rarely know what is best for all the people in relationship to serving humanity and humanity's needs.

But here is the good news: there are a percentage of souls on this planet called starseed who are older souls, and if you get that astral (past-life) experience and spirituality mixed together in a man or woman, you have the beginning of a great leader. The greatest leaders in the history of the world have usually been starseed. Here is a very small list of starseed leaders of the last few hundred years who challenged the established thought-systems with something more evolved: Martin Luther, Teresa of Avila, Oliver Cromwell, George Washington, Thomas Jefferson, Baha'u'llah, Nelson Mandela, Hildegard Von Bingham, Benazir Bhutto, John and Robert Kennedy, Aung San Suu Kyi, and many more.

Other great leaders who are new souls are: Martin Luther King, Jr., Stephen Biko, Ken Saro Wiwa, Gandhi, and President Jimmy Carter, to name a few. All five of these men had to deal with the fallen system and the 1%, and new souls do not fare as well but they still make great accomplishments, although they are often more manipulated by starseed leaders in office. Many of these new souls can accomplish what they do because they have starseed genetics from their ancestors. See *The Cosmic Family, Volume I*.

Until the people's spiritual eyes are opened to know who these great leaders are in contemporary times, the people will often choose the wrong ones. The real leaders are usually oppressed by the system and misrepresented, because the 1% does not want them "out there" with the truth. Often the only medium these elder leaders have is the Internet or books they can get published, via print-on-demand. As I mentioned in a previous article, even Free Speech TV and Link TV play it safe and do not let speakers who rock the boat too much (particularly bringing in spirituality) in their programming. After all, they are licensed by the FCC—the Federal Communications Commission. And often they go too far to the left, into relativity, and have programs where anything goes.

You also cannot look for these leaders at established churches, particularly nondenominational Christian fundamentalist churches. I would look more towards the more liberal groups in Christianity and other religious persuasions. These leaders probably have left the system a long time ago and are either the head of intentional communities or a member of one. They usually gravitate to subcultures, and many are artists like musicians, painters, sculptors, and entrepreneurs, like Elon Musk, Co-Founder of PayPal, who started SpaceX, and Richard Branson, who started Virgin Records and now Virgin Galactic, a space tourism company. However, the majority of starseed are not interested so much in making money as in bringing cutting-edge ideas to the world.

You will not usually be able to find them in the New Age movement either because too many in that movement deny the existence of a personal Creator. And even if these individuals were in the New Age for a while, it probably was when they were much younger and realized that without having a truly spiritualized mind in relationship with the Creator, higher truths cannot be found. Much of the New Age teachings have a lot of relativity and deny absolutes.

All higher spiritual seekers discover that there is relativity within absoluteness but not absoluteness in relativity. In other words, a leader must have a sense of the absoluteness of right and wrong within divine law and pattern in order to make the highest decisions pertaining to a multitude of situations where relativity is then applied.

When only relativity guides someone in leadership, there is no foundation of absoluteness in ethics, morality, and spirituality that guide them in making decisions in everyday circumstantial reality, thus many decisions are arbitrary and lack wisdom or foresight and are based on selfish and often immoral and unethical motives. As civilization advances, higher regulatory moral conduct has to be written within laws that govern a vast variety of people who make up the masses of modern civilization that have now reached the hundreds of millions in some countries and billions in others.

In the kingdom of God there is no competition. There is only understanding and the knowledge within one's self that another person is more spiritually qualified to govern than you are. The thirst for power blinds most candidates for office. If understanding and spiritual discernment guided individuals running for office, there would not have to be elections, or if there are elections, there would be no dirty politics that come with campaigning. The most spiritually-advanced individual should have the position, and all candidates should know that.

If they would have recognized Jesus Christ, who was the Son of God, they would not have crucified Him. But the 1% have never been about recognizing true leaders—spiritual or otherwise—and they have always come against them with their police or armies and misrepresented them with the media of the time.

On a fallen world like Earth, wise understanding and discernment within the spiritualized mind are not there among the majority of leaders. Many in the younger generation are now beginning to have eyes to see this. That is why the Occupy movement is happening, not just in this country but all over the world. No form of government has worked in its greatest potential on this planet in the last 200,000 years since the Lucifer Rebellion. Great ideals have led many a revolution, but these revolutions all fell to greedy rulers who control the masses, no matter what that form of government was called.

Only with a Divine Administration, on a planetary level, can true peace and justice come to this planet. That is why people all over the world are crying out for change and revolution. But what they all have not realized yet is that it will take a Spiritualution movement to solve the problems of their country and the rest of the world. In all of these countries and religions of the world, their scriptural texts speak of a coming of a Promised One, who will rule and reign and bring peace to the earth.

Many of the young people of these countries and religions do not even know that this teaching is in their religions, because they have not yet gotten into their own religions enough. However, the real thing that they have to get into is not actually their religions but to become better human beings—human beings who treat others as they want to be treated, human beings who practice love toward all humankind, human beings who do not see colors of races with prejudiced eyes but see only other brothers and sisters.

True spirituality is not about being born again in a fundamentalist religion that perceives that its way is the only way to reach eternity. It is not about being "washed in the blood of Christ" but actually about understanding what Christ taught about love. It is not about accepting the doctrines of man of any of these religions. It is about the freedom to freely worship the Creator in whatever way we see fit, without someone telling us that were not "saved" if we do not do it the way they do.

The Spiritualution, the spiritual revolution, is about actively fighting against evil wherever it is found, actively seeking justice for all the peoples of the planet (not just for yourself and your own group, whatever that group may be). It is about using your talents for the common good of all, not just yourself or the corporation you work for. Your use of talents has to go much further than your employer. It has to reach out to all humanity. That is why the Creator gave you these talents.

In my numerous articles, I have spoken about these things in various ways, but often—unfortunately on this fallen world, with people trapped in fallen systems of thought—the same truth has to be said in many ways before a person really gets it. A lot of the middle-class apathy-ites and definitely the 1% do not want to get it. What? Love run this planet rather than greed? Giving run this planet rather than taking? Equal opportunity for all run this planet? Taking to the streets to peacefully protest rather than turning a blind eye to oppression?

Many people have these good thoughts, but they brush them off because they feel it can never happen, that it is too idealistic. And so they back off into a safe corner of their minds and hearts and never do anything to change anything. That is why the 1% have kept the rule for many centuries over the 99%, because unfortunately many in the 99% are the apathy-ites. It is mostly the young adults and some teens wise beyond their years (and most of them starseed) in America who are now beginning to take to the streets and are starting to cry out for true freedom instead of bondage to the 1% and the system of greed.

In other countries life is much more difficult, but life in America, Canada, England, Germany, and basically the Anglo-Saxon countries is still very comfortable for so many citizens. That will change because more and more people will wake up (particularly the parents of the young out on the streets) and start to scream too, like they are doing in Syria and Yemen and Egypt and Libya and Bahrain and Burma, where thousands of monks marched with the people in protest. People in these countries definitely have their own Spiritualution movement going on. The Spiritualution movement is transnational and transreligious and preaches no particular religious doctrines, but it does encourage active civil disobedience against the world's 1% oppressors.

The 1% controls the 99%, but the people who suffer most are the Third World countries in which people live in squalor, malnutrition, hunger, and disease with no hope of ever getting out of their forced-upon circumstances. Here in America 90 million Americans (as of 2007) live under the poverty level. This is according to Bob Herbert, "The Millions Left Out," *New York Times*, May 12, 2007. With the present economic situation in America, this figure probably is even higher. Poverty, on material as well as spiritual levels, is the reason for drugs, violence, and crime. Where there is no hope, there is no future. And it is written, "Where there is no vision, the people perish."

In the beginning of the American Revolution in the 1770s, the uprising began within the churches. The pastors were the leaders. They spoke out for moral reasons against the British imperialism. They created a form of Spiritualution movement. They did not call it that, but that is what it was. It is too bad they had to pick up arms to win against oppression of the American people by the Crown of England, the 1%. But the first shots were fired by the British.

In the recent celebration of the sixty-year reign of Queen Elizabeth II, called the Diamond Jubilee, millions of people cheered while the elite (dressed to the hilt in their military uniforms and opulence) drove by. The majority of these millions of people do not even realize their oppression. They have settled for less in their lives than what the Creator would want for their destinies. They have settled for less for the destinies of their own children and grandchildren.

If you are questioning what some of the concepts mean that I am talking about, you can study more about them in depth in my books *The Divine New Order And The Dawn Of The First Stage Of Light And Life* and *The Cosmic Family* volumes.

On this earth we have not even evolved to seeing ourselves as planetary citizens. We are still very much into nationalism. Nationalism continues to divide one group of people from another. According to *The URANTIA Book* and *The Cosmic Family* volumes, an evolutionary planet with various races and creeds has to come to a place where we see each other as planetary brothers and sisters, not as it is now with approximately 196 countries in competition for political power and the earth's resources. All races of color can intermarry and amalgamate eventually into one race with one common language so that we can understand each other and still appreciate our uniqueness as individuals. (There may still be other languages among the diversity of peoples, but all people can also speak a common language.)

The divisions on this planet are many and seemingly insurmountable, particularly religious differences on the nature of God. But peace will never come to this planet unless all human beings everywhere begin to adopt true spiritual change within themselves and begin to see the world with spiritual eyes. This is the Spiritualution movement that is so needed all over this world, and this is what people are really crying out for, one person at a time.

It can begin with you. Are you willing to change your viewpoints that may be wrong? Are you willing to think of the betterment of other people other than yourself? Are you willing to unoccupy your couch and do what you can to change this world? And if you have, and now possibly have taken to the streets, perhaps you have to unoccupy your minds of old thinking to embrace higher truth and more higher concepts of planetary ordinances, statutes, laws, and conduct for a new civilization of peace and justice for this planet. As has been emphasized by many wise spiritual leaders over the centuries: you need to be the change.

To Achieve Cultural And Religious Unity In A One-World Government Outside Of The Control Of The 1%, A Global Spiritualution Is The Only Answer

I personally believe that there should be no borders anywhere on the earth and that we are all planetary citizens, in actuality one planetary family. I coined the phrase in the 1990s "One God, One Planetary Family." The power elite or the 1% would want a different kind of one world government for their own greedy and power-hungry reasons, so that negative movement is already happening within the echelons of the rich and powerful controllers.

However, there is another movement going on that is the movement of the people, the 99% of the world, who are crying out for true freedom and true justice for the people. That is what a Spiritualution is: worldwide justice for the people, a spiritual awakening, the understanding that we are all children under the same Creator and that we need to get away from the "isms" that divide us within those religious dogmas and fundamentalism. *The Urantia Book* emphasizes that the highest ideal is "unity without uniformity."

Norms are needed within a culture in order to have some commonality and unity among the people. When people do not have those norms, anomie takes place, and people feel uprooted and scattered. To use a simple example, some people in some countries wave goodbye by the hand going up and down away from the face, while in other countries by the hand going backwards towards the face. Both gestures mean the same thing: goodbye, but if that is not known, then misunderstanding and miscommunication can occur.

At the same time, it would be terrible to have sameness in all cultures, a world monoculture. When we allow for differences and understand those differences, other cultures do not seem so strange, and thus more appreciation and cooperation is possible. Throughout history the problem has been that when imperialism (or some other form of "conquering") takes place, the invading nation tries to force people of other cultures to all think, act, and dress the same way, leaving no room for diversity.

In actuality, only moral codes that determine rightness and wrongness in almost all circumstances should be universal. But even there, they too differ in various cultures. I think humanity can all agree upon a few of them: that we should not murder each other, steal from each other, be jealous of each other's successes, be resentful, be greedy or selfish, and be unforgiving. But most all other areas are a multitude of different opinions of what moral issues are. So trying to get everybody on the earth to abide by international cultural standardization is not going to be an easy matter. For example, with the recent summer Olympics some countries have no problem with women volleyball players playing in bikinis whereas many Moslem countries think dressing in bikinis is immoral, therefore their women cannot enter the games because they dress more modestly.

These gray areas of morality cannot be legislated, like many religious fundamentalists want to do in almost all countries. Millions of Americans have voted into office individuals that they think are godly, and half of the rest of the country think that they are not godly or moral. Those differences of opinion can be a good thing! But the fact that ungodly, unethical people get into office by democratic vote, that is a bad thing, because if you have the majority of the masses who cannot discern who is the real thing and who are the phonies, chaos will continue.

This is why only through a Spiritualution happening within individual people—when people begin to want to change themselves and become more perfect spiritually—can they discern for themselves those who come only in the name of God and those who truly walk in the will of God. Actions truly do speak louder than words.

In Taoism, the understanding that good and evil exist together and that good can contain some evil and evil contain some good may be true. But until human beings learn to tip the scale of their own lives into the plus/good area, they will be worthless as servants of humanity and so-called "Ministers of State," because they will make more mistakes out of their own greed and quest for dio (evil) power than for altruistic and humanitarian reasons.

In Buddhism there is a word, engi, which conveys the understanding that everything is related. The Sioux nation has the phrase mitakuye oyasin that means the same thing, "all my relations." The depth of this concept of interrelatedness is immense in its implications, but basically it indicates that we are all responsible for what we do as well as what we fail to do.

Some quantum physicists even think that objects have an energy that spreads not only across continents but across planets and universes. Therefore, negative thoughts have their negative effects. In *The Cosmic Family, Volume I*, these negative energies are called distortion and delusion energies that cause dysfunctional thinking within people, which is part of the reason why people today are mass-killing other people.

When enough people within any one location are thinking below the standard norm for human decency, these negative energies act as a kind of negative force field that spins mentally unstable and emotionally imbalanced people to commit acts of violence against themselves or others. It is mostly men who commit these violent acts, due to various factors.

One of the factors is that men have an innate instinct of desiring a mate and children that they will be responsible for. In most cultures today that means success in manifesting an income to provide support and protection for the family. With the added pressures in modern society of the need for additional prestige and an image of success, many young men do go crazy who think they cannot meet the criteria of what their society is asking of them. Therefore, in this sense, an international norm of cultural understanding has to be accepted in relationship to what true success is, which does not place so much emphasis on making more money than necessary in providing a sustainable living for a family. There also should be an international standard of pay in all fields that allows for the family to exist if only the male is working.

There is innate in all human beings the desire for recognition of one's talents, abilities, and accomplishments, no matter what they may be. Some people can be happy on a job doing manual labor, while others would need to use their minds more. So in keeping in line with the Hindi word sukha, there needs to be an international understanding of "sukha" in employment, because workers need to feel pleasurable, joyful, agreeable, easy, comfortable, happy, prosperous, and relaxed, as opposed to duhkuh, which is mental discomfort, suffering or pain caused by unhappiness on the job.

In Hinduism the word Kshatriya constitutes the military and ruling elite of the Vedic-Hindu social system, the 1% of their culture. But Jesus said that "the meek [humble] will inherit the earth," which is quite a contrast to the attitude that "might is right." Humanity has to begin to recognize its true spiritual elders or else the majority will continue to be controlled by and (in some manner) slaves of the 1%. There needs to be a Spiritualution of thinking in order to be able to discern what true humility is and is not in a person, especially in political, social, and religious leaders.

Most Americans do not even know they are supposed to look for that value of humility in a leader. They have been taught by the movies of the Hollywood delusion and propaganda that the tough guy or macho man or rich and powerful person is the best equipped to lead. Even thousands of years ago the people of Israel cried out to give them Saul as their leader and king because he was very tall, which indicated to them power, but God chose David to be the future king, who was small in stature but humble in heart and big in faith and vision. David had a true heart and spiritized mind to serve the people.

In Hinduism there are the Brahmins—the class of artists, priests, intellectuals, scientists, and visionaries who are highly esteemed. In other societies, artists, poets, writers, and visionaries are not thought of so highly and often struggle to make a living with their talents. As a matter of fact, when revolutions take place in many countries, often the poets, writers, painters, and even musicians are the first ones to be killed because they have the potential power through their talents to reach the masses.

People begin to fear each other when one side is less godly than the other or the whole country becomes very materialistic or even anti-God. The answer to these kinds of divisions is, again, a Spiritualution, where people evolve out of wrong perceptions of the Creator, which is usually the interpretation of the 1%, who define a god of fear and wrath. In Spiritualution thinking, the revolutionaries of consciousness begin to see many of their own problems and imbalances as a result of the cause and effect of their wrong thinking and their wrong decisions rather than a wrathful God who is ready to squash them in punishment by giving them problems and tragedies. Spiritualution thinking realizes that God does not punish people who do something against someone else's moral standards, particularly the moral standards and dogma of fundamentalists in any religion.

These consciousness revolutionaries begin to see themselves as planetary citizens, not just belonging to one particular country but the country of the global community of the world. As they begin to walk more and more away from their evolutionary religious viewpoints, their 1% leadership begins to get angry and come against them by making life harder for them, passing new laws that control the people, give less privacy, make it harder for people to communicate with each other, make it harder for people to travel (particularly around the world). Only the rich and sons and daughters of the rich can travel easily internationally. Most human beings never even leave their own local geographic area all their lives. Even a lot of Americans never have been to another state, let alone another country.

Education has always been controlled by the 1%. The 1% needs a lot of servants to run their mansions. Even today the most expensive universities are only attended by the upper middle class and rich, and only token scholarships are given to the poor, so that the universities can say they are nondiscriminatory and their universities are open to everybody.

In Hinduism there is a word for the merchants called Vaishya, which in India, in order to make any kind of decent living, a person has to be at least in this class, which is like a middle class. In Western civilization too, the merchants have had to sell a lot of wares/products to remain in the middle class or even become the upper middle class of their culture. Today the small, independent businessman in retail can hardly exist due to large corporations controlling the market, which leads to the decline of a civilization in all areas, including morally.

If goods are made cheaply and quickly (as is usually the case with large, corporate-owned companies), they are less valuable and can be mass-produced. Of course it does not matter if the merchandise falls apart, because you can always buy another "it," and so why should the craftsmen spend the time to make anything long-lasting with design and quality if people can buy the duplicate one of less quality for half the price? It is a throw-away world, and craftsmanship, art, and creativity have also been thrown away.

It has been a lot harder for artists to earn a living, particularly musicians, because the corporate-controlled music industry is for most singers and instrumentalists who can sing and play by rote, most sounding the same. Sadly, the young people growing up do not even know what a good instrumentalist or singer should sound like. It is the same thing in painting, and so Andy Warhol could become famous and he paints tomato cans.

Automobiles used to be made of steel and chrome but are now made with plastic. As a result, more people are killed in car accidents now when cars hit each other because there is no protection for people inside because the plastic bumpers and doors just crumble or cave in. So in this throw-away world, in automobile manufacturing, design and quality have also been thrown away.

Too many people think they have to compromise and work in these factories that create "fast," cheaply produced products to make a living—be it automobiles, boats, clothes, appliances, and even building materials—because all the companies owned by the 1% mass-produce junk products.

The answer to this madness of mediocrity is the Spiritualution, because part of the Spiritualution message is cooperation with each other to survive sustainably. Today many people are caught in the system of striving for mere materialistic survival, but cooperation has always been and should be for reasons of creativity—to create quality lives and by-products. So reasons you should leave a society that does not work anymore today and join with others is not just for your mere survival, but to be able to use your talents and abilities to create together quality products of lasting usefulness and beauty. Living and working in cooperation with like-minded people not only creates quality things but also quality lives.

In Islam there's a term called sura, which means "solidarity." Americans and Europeans need to learn the meaning of solidarity with each other again in so many walks of life, because the 1% does not want solidarity among people; they want division. Actually, the Aquarian Age that we are coming into—with its Aquarian energies and Aquarian concepts—is an age of cooperation with each other. Division began 200,000 years ago when the system sovereign of Satania, Lucifer (a primary Lanonandek Son, according to *The URANTIA Book*), created division in the minds and hearts of the mortals and celestial beings under his influence.

"Divide and conquer" started in this rebellion on the earth, and those with greed in their hearts throughout time have used this as their greatest strategy and weapon of control over the masses. Today the power is in the hands of the 1% because of the wealth they control. They have been able to divide and compartmentalize humanity into religions, political systems, racism, nationalism, corporate identity, ethnocentrism, dress codes, educational degrees, and many other ideologies.

Cultural globalization cannot occur until a true Spiritualution takes place, and that, again, is humanity seeing ourselves as one planetary family under one Creator. That is the first step. We have to get away from metacultures, where people are ranked by class, financial status, educational degrees, and careers (such as Hollywood starlet or rock star statuses). Who is more important when you have a major leak in your plumbing and your house is flooding, a doctor or a plumber? Who is more important when your car breaks down, an attorney or a mechanic? Who is smarter, the baker or the stockbroker? Who is more intelligent, the airline pilot or the construction worker?

The idea of IQ tests is a moot point in many situations. When you need someone to help build your house, you do not ask or try to hire an airplane pilot. Particularly in Western civilization we seem to have categorized "smartness" by what a man or women does for a living. We categorize people "successful" by how they make a living and how much money they earn. In Spiritualution thinking, you begin to see people as equals, no matter what they do for a living, therefore breaking down the age-old caste systems in our consciousness and creating a global consciousness of equality. We must remember that Jesus was a carpenter, and this is how He made His living. But He was also a very learned man in many disciplines.

In diachronic thinking, because these caste and class systems have been around for so many hundreds and thousands of years, there is a global, regional, and cultural judgment of each other within those cultures and outside of them, which I will term "frozen devaluation." In *The Cosmic Family* volumes it speaks of the future society, for a time, being separated into sectors of consciousness. In a way, even now in parts of the United States and other countries—particularly in Western civilization—there have been (for hundreds of years) the arts area of a city where the "bohemians" hang out in order to communicate artistic, social, and political concepts with each other, in what they felt was a more communicative atmosphere of understanding.

It is not that the scientists—who are more "left-brained"—cannot also be artistic, but the way our education systems are structured, people become specialists in one area and inadequate in many others. I believe that the human brain has the capacity to learn many things, and education should be structured to develop the whole brain, not just 10% of it.

Another tenet in Spiritualution thinking is that a career is something that we may be doing at one particular time in our lives, but it is not who we are, and we may have more than one career as we develop and grow. Many people may be great writers or musicians or architects or whatever but never get an opportunity to do that because they have to earn a living at something else due to life circumstances where they have been placed in a field other than where their real talent lies. That is why so many people are depressed and destroy themselves through alcohol and drugs.

To reiterate, none of these changes can be accomplished through violence. It has to be an inward change of each and every human being towards a consciousness of radical unity in every possible way. Using the Buddhist principle of ahimsa (nonviolence) to change the thinking of the wrong policies of governmental leaders and mass consciousness is the same principle that Jesus taught when He said to turn the other cheek when someone hits you. Force cannot change someone's mind if that mind is on the side of the police force or if the mind is on the side of anarchists.

Gandhi and Martin Luther King, Jr. were able to practice nonviolent resistance and change the mass consciousness of a country, but both of these men were also spiritual leaders. Both of these men started a Spiritualution in their own countries. Unfortunately, both of these men were murdered by their own countrymen, because often change for the masses comes very slowly, even though the raison d'être that they were actively trying to change was partially accomplished before they died. India did get its independence from Britain, but Gandhi did not want the partition of two countries—the Muslims in Pakistan and the Hindus in India—but a united country for all Indians, regardless of race or religion. Martin Luther King, Jr. wanted equal opportunity for the black race in America, which in reality took another almost fifty years before a black President was elected.

Change happens slowly unless millions of individuals make that inner change of consciousness together. If that would have been the case in both of those movements, Gandhi and Martin Luther King, Jr. would not have been assassinated, because the Deo (godly) power of the mass consciousness would have prevented it. If many more people had been aligned in supporting the work of these two men, their positive thoughts and actions would have set up an energy that could have prevented the negative forces behind the evil deeds of murdering these two great leaders.

These are spiritual principles that only a few in the New Age and those in other spiritual walks of life understand. But a quantum leap of consciousness needs to take place on this planet in order to speak to the elements of the earth, so that the worldwide weather patterns can come back to normal, because if they do not, the earth will be destroyed by the negativity of the thoughts of the billions of people on the planet who are now propagandized every day by the 1%'s bombardment of the teachings of greed and moral decay through the mass media they control.

The 1%'s mass media worldwide bombardment has touched every country, including China, Japan, India, African nations, and South American countries. The moral breakdown of these countries has happened at the rate that these countries allow

American television, films, and magazines to propagandize their people. Only some of the Moslem countries are standing firmer against the 1%'s influence in advertising to their citizens. However, they have their own 1% who controls their people, often in cahoots with AmericanF interests. And they have their own backward fundamentalist dogma that holds people back from attaining better lives.

When The Promised One returns, will He be Christian? Hindu? Buddhist? Of Islam or Judaism? Will He be white? Or black? Or yellow? Or red? Will He be of the upper classes? Of course not! And for those of us who are still stuck in the lower consciousness of our minds, that separate us from each other in human compassion, we will have to go to the spiritual elementary schools of learning how to accept one another as brothers and sisters, equal in the eyes of the Creator.

UPDATE: September 20, 2012

On Tuesday September 17, 2012 my 22-year-old son Amadon was arrested and spent eleven hours in jail at the One-Year Anniversary of Occupy Wall Street at Zuccotti Park in New York City. There were more than 200 arrests that day—a lot of live streamers, who the police seemed to target. Amadon was warned once about climbing up on a light post to try take pictures of the crowd but not warned several times, like the officer said on the film we have when Amadon was being taken to the paddy wagon and was inside of it. The police know how to protect themselves when they're on camera, and they actually took Amadon's camera and let it run while they made these statements to protect themselves. They confiscated the Spiritualution banner and would not give it back. Funny, you would think that they would want the message of Spiritualution to be seen in these demonstrations, as it is a message of peaceful demonstration and for people to have spiritual consciousness, like Gandhi, Martin Luther King, Jr., and myself taught (as well as, of course, Jesus Christ who first taught the message).

Amadon was in jail with an 81-year-old pastor, as well as two other pastors. I wonder what this 81-year-old pastor did. I don't think that he could climb up onto much of anything. Amadon was charged with two charges: 'disorderly conduct' and 'reckless endangerment.' On the endangerment charge, if they don't dismiss it, Amadon can actually get a year in jail. The National Lawyers Guild of America is on it as soon as someone is arrested, and they take the names of the persons arrested and represent them in court. Amadon is set for trial on December 5, 2012 and will speak by phone to New York (from Arizona). Amadon has only ever gotten one speeding ticket for going six miles over the speed limit, does not use drugs or alcohol, and has spoken out against any kind of anarchism to the anarchists in many cities where he has gone to the Occupy events, and, of course, lives in a spiritual community. Let us hope and pray that the New York Police do the right thing and drop this second charge and that Amadon is not just another one of their targets to make an example of.

Global Interdependence Day
July 5th

I propose that every July 5th the Occupy movement needs to celebrate a Global Interdependence Day to help the 99% realize our interdependence upon one another, and to help us get away from nationalism and see ourselves as world citizens. Global Interdependence Day should be held on the 5th of July (after the 4th of July) to represent a new order of thinking.

How Do You Choose To Occupy This World?
by Niánn Emerson Chase

I have read numerous well-written, thoughtful, educational, and inspiring articles about the Occupy movement in this country by Occupiers and those who identify with the 99% movement. Some of these people are well-known and highly respected academics and award-winning writers, and many are highly knowledgeable and intelligent young people who do not want the future that the corporate-controlled rulers of this world have laid out for them. I have also read quite a few diatribes against the Occupy movement, accusing it of being nothing but an unorganized group of washed-out hippies, the homeless, and rebellious young people who do not even know what they want. And I have met several people who still do not know much at all about the Occupy movement (and could care less), because they are so wrapped up in just getting by in their own struggles to have a life.

What I do know is that for several months the Occupy movement was a fast-moving "happening," in spite of the attempts to diminish its importance by the corporate-controlled mainstream media. Now, unfortunately, due to the corporately-directed political strategists who use the local governments and police to do their dirty work, the movement has slowed down across the country due to so many of the Occupiers being evicted from the parks and other places where they were camped. But the ideas of the Occupiers are still actively being promoted in other ways, so the movement continues.

I live in a state that has been nationally ranked as one of the top five states who have the most number of poor people living in them (per capita). I live in a county that is counted as one of the three poorest counties in the state. So, when I come across the more financially privileged and politically conservative people in my neck of the woods (actually desert) who deride me and my associates for counting ourselves as part of the 99%, I scratch my head in puzzlement and frustration at what I consider ignorance and an unwillingness to really look at all of the facts and truth of the state of our nation and world, and here in Arizona, the state of our fellow Arizonians—many who happen to be red (Native American) and brown (Hispanic) and suspected of being "illegal" and "alien."

I grew up on Native American reservations in a very "middle" middle-class family who, more than fifty years ago, recycled everything we could, conserved in our energy and water usage, and spent money carefully and conservatively. We lived a life of considerate compassion and respect for all human beings and had a scientific and spiritual appreciation for the web of life on our planet. (My father was a soil conservationist, a spiritual man, and loved the natural world.) We did not buy new cars and kept the used ones for at least ten years, even up to twenty years, because my father maintained them so carefully. Like my parents before me, I still purchase most of my clothing, furniture, and other household items in thrift stores and resale shops. I, as well as most of my family, friends, and close associates, have never come near being one of those crazed shopping-spree enthusiasts who trample people to get into a store to buy the latest item that is faddish on the much-promoted "Black Friday" shopping day after Thanksgiving. So, according to the constant jangle from most economists, I guess we are not doing our part in helping the economy recover.

I was blessed to grow up without a television and have continued to resist being brain-stained and tantalized into personally identifying with corporate brand names, labels, and logos that are crammed down our throats through invasive, mass advertising that comes at us from all directions through multiple-media formats. Even while we are pumping gasoline at a gas station we are subjected to inane chatter trying to sell us something from a small video box sitting on top of the damn gasoline pump! It seems that most of us have to tramp back into a designated wilderness area to get away from corporate occupation of our lives.

Many of my childhood friends did not even have running water or electricity in their one- or two-room homes that housed large families, let alone other commodities that most of us in this country today take for granted. In that setting, I guess my family and I were the 1%, but unlike the nation's 1% referred to in the Occupy Wall Street and 99% movements, my family and I were not taking anything away from our neighbors and friends or living beyond our means at the expense of the majority of our fellow planetary citizens and neighbors. We were where we were to share our knowledge and lives with our friends and neighbors who lived below the poverty level of the times, in order to assist them to become part of the middle class—in their housing, healthcare, education, economics, and lifestyles.

Unfortunately, more than fifty years later, not much has really changed for Native Americans when it comes to quality and dignity of life. Though some have more money and material things, the quality of their education and healthcare has not improved much, and neither has the quality of their psychospiritual well-being. But neither has the quality of most American's psychospiritual well-being improved in the last fifty years, regardless of race or economic status. And why is that? Because of the increasing acceptance of toxic materialism as a way of life—a materialism that values money and power over human beings and our life-giving natural world. Unfortunately, now, the gains in education and healthcare that Americans had acquired in the last fifty years are also being taken away.

As those of us involved in the Occupy movement realize, we live in a world that is ruled by corporations who control political policies, practices, and laws and in an economic system that is dependent upon all of us—who are poor or of the presently-dwindling middle-class or even of the more economically privileged group—to spend as much money as we can, living way beyond our financial means, which is one of the factors that has contributed to the plummet into this terrible economic recession.

All of us Americans have been occupied by the corporate rhetoric that brain-stains us to buy, buy, buy—whether we need it or not, and without consideration of the cost to other human beings, other cultures, and the natural world that sustains all of our lives. We are intoxicated by the constant barrage of propaganda that comes at us through corporate-controlled media to grab a bigger piece of the pie, use our talents and knowledge for getting more money, prestige, and power. We are constantly being coerced to be selfish, fearful, grasping citizens in order to serve the current economy and the less-than-one percent that is the machine running the materialistic world. We are considered failures and become social outcasts of the mainstream if we choose another value-system, one that rejects getting more than we need and questions those who continue to feed the machine that is methodically destroying our beautiful natural world, our diverse cultures, decent values, ethical practices, and the well-being of us humans.

I live in a spiritually-based EcoVillage with about one hundred others who have occupied part of the borderlands in Southern Arizona. We have chosen a simpler life that challenges anything and anyone that damages the human soul and psyche, diminishes the higher ideals of a truly sustainable culture and society, and destroys the delicate yet sustaining web of life that makes up the natural world. We have chosen to occupy this planet in a manner that celebrates life, living daily in a manner that constantly strives for a more compassionate, scientific, and spiritualized perspective and lifestyle. We are religionists, environmentalists, educators, organic gardeners and farmers, artists, musicians, writers, parents, healthcare providers, and so on. And we piss comfortable people off, because we have occupied their comfort zones of complacency and greedy grabbing.

We are part of the Occupy movement in our daily thinking, doing, and being. We join hundreds of thousands of others in this country and millions across the planet who demand a more sustainable and decent life for all human beings and for all of life. Our EcoVillage and organic gardens, farm, and ranch are a functioning sustainable model that serves as a prototype and proof that a few good people working in harmony together and for the common good of all can make a real difference in changing the tides of greed, in any pocket of the world. We, like all Occupiers, do this through our talking, our writings, our public events, our educating, our music, our art, and, most importantly, through our own personal changes in consciousness and lifestyle.

Regardless of nationality, political creed, racial identity, economical status, religious (or otherwise) affiliation, or ideology, all of us Occupiers across the planet need to continue holding the dream of a much better life for all, and, even more importantly, to actually stand up for and actualize that dream daily in our own personal lives and the lives of our neighbors, as part of a huge planetary Spiritualu-tion^{SM} movement that is unfolding every day.

This article was originally published in the Spring 2012 issue ("Occupy! — Where Do We Go From Here?") of the Alternative Voice *quarterly periodical*

The following three articles were written by staff of Global Change Multi-Media, who have traveled to Occupy events in several U.S. cities (listed below), and were originally published in the Spring 2012 issue ("Occupy! — Where Do We Go From Here?") of the Alternative Voice *quarterly periodical.*

Occupy Wall Street
Zuccotti Park, New York City
October 10–11, 2011

Occupy Tucson/March on the Banks
Armory Park, Tucson, Arizona
October 15 & November 5, 2011

Occupy ALEC
Scottsdale (Phoenix), Arizona
November 30, 2011

Occupy Phoenix/March with Jesse Jackson
Phoenix, Arizona
December 1, 2011

West Coast Port Blockade
Long Beach, California
December 12, 2011

March On The L.A.P.D.
Los Angeles, California
December 12–13, 2011

Occupy Green Valley
Green Valley, Arizona
December 15, 2011

Occupy Congress
Washington, D.C.
January 17, 2012

NATO Protest
Chicago, Illinois
May 20–21, 2012

Occupy National Gathering
Philadelphia, Pennsylvania
June 30–July 4, 2012

The Anaheim March Against Police Brutality
Anaheim, California
July 29, 2012

One-Year Anniversary of Occupy Wall Street
New York City
September 15–17, 2012

The Occupy Movement Needs Leadership Now

by BenDameean Steinhardt

Much of the concepts within this article are inspired by the writings by Gabriel of Urantia.

I have traveled with my friends of Global Change Multi-Media to several Occupy cities including New York, Los Angeles, and Tucson, participating in marches, protests, and general assemblies. Before Bloomberg's Gestapo forced out the Wall Street Occupiers, I spent time at Zuccotti Park in New York City and experienced the passion and hope of thousands of activists who had gathered from around the country and world to stand up against a system that kowtows to the 1% at the expense of the 99%. It was inspiring to see so many people of all ages and walks of life coming together to protest injustice with the belief that their voices and actions could make a difference in bringing a new day to our planet. My friends and I also marched at "Occupy The Ports" in L.A. and subsequently have participated in many other Occupy events in Tucson, Phoenix, and Washington D.C. at Occupy Congress.

The Occupy movement is at a crossroads. It can either diminish, which seems to be the course it is on, or it can potentially evolve into a world-changing movement that can defeat the 1% and eventually lead to true freedom and justice for all. In order to have a chance of achieving the latter, the

Occupy movement must change its thinking concerning leadership. It is the current lack of leadership within the Occupy movement that will keep it from reaching its greatest potential.

A "leaderless movement"—as the Occupy movement proclaims itself to be, where decisions are made by the process of "consensus" through "People's Assemblies" and where both "no one is a leader" and "everyone is a leader"—may have worked in the beginning stages when there were fewer numbers. But now that the Occupy movement has spread like wildfire around the United States and world, the "leaderless" aspect and process of "consensus" has proven to be an inefficient and disorganized way to guide and unite masses of people and is holding back the progress of the movement. It is a matter of common sense that a higher form of leadership and organization is now needed to take the Occupy movement to the next phase.

A lack of leadership and management in a movement leads to a lack of organization and focus. A lack of organization and focus leads to a lack of motivation and efficiency. When there is a lack of organization, focus, motivation, and efficiency, a movement lacks unity and flounders, losing its power. This is what is happening with the Occupy movement. Strong leadership is needed within the 99% to galvanize its protesters and to create levels of management where individuals have specific responsibilities and roles. Without somebody saying "this is what we need to do," very little gets done. Good leadership motivates and inspires the best in others and gives people a sense of united empowerment that is missing in the Occupy movement.

I experienced this firsthand at Occupy events I took part in, where, because of a lack of leadership and organization, people were not clear about what to do or where to go, thus most of the protests we were participating in did not feel unified and imbued with a strong sense of purpose. The Occupy movements across the country should be working together much more effectively to mobilize the 99% en masse, but it seems like the right hand does not know what the left hand is doing. It is of course important to continue carrying out direct actions locally, but the Occupy movements nationwide must support each other and unite by forming a national leadership council to coordinate and communicate their plans and goals. The movement must focus on planning national actions and events that will truly impact the pocketbooks of the 1% and draw masses of Occupiers from around the country that will show the power of the 99%. The more unified the movement is, the stronger it will be, and the more people it will draw.

Don't get me wrong; I consider myself an Occupier, and I love the Occupy movement and what it stands for, but I want to see this movement realize its full potential. I acknowledge that the process of consensus through General Assemblies has its admirable qualities such as the ability to empower people to express themselves and participate in collective decision making. But when this process takes hours upon hours to make trivial decisions that could have been made in five minutes, it begins to have a paralyzing effect.

Any great movement in history has been spearheaded by strong and wise leadership, visionary men and women who were servants of people and had a relationship to a greater power than themselves. To keep a movement going forward, eventually there need to be individuals who take command and responsibility for motivating, leading, and organizing others that the consensus process just does not provide. Critical decisions often must be made in the moment, and there need to be leaders who have earned the right through their experience and virtue to make those decisions. Plublilius Syrus, a Latin writer in the first century B.C. said, "The greater a man is in power above others, the more he ought to excel them in virtue. None ought to govern who is not better than the governed."

I acknowledge that a "leaderless" movement where "there are no leaders" and simultaneously "everyone is a leader" is very attractive to people. The only problem is that it does not work. Indeed, we are all called to be leaders as the Occupy movement professes. However, if there are too many "chiefs" then there are not enough people to carry out the nuts-and-bolts implementation of the vision. In order to become a good leader, one must learn to follow. Aristotle proclaimed, "He who has never learned to obey cannot be a good commander."

I can understand why the Occupy movement decided to be "leaderless" and ascribe to the process of consensus. People are rightly disgusted by our corrupt government and its false leaders who are bought and paid for by greedy corporations and who have abused the authority vested in them. The Occupy movement's fear of leadership, management, and hierarchy is understandable because of the appallingly unprincipled example so-called leaders and governments have set over the past several decades. Real leadership is so rare on this planet that people do not even know what it is anymore. Robert F. Kennedy had it right when he said, "The problem of power is how to achieve its responsible use rather than its irresponsible and indulgent use—how to get men of power to live for the public rather than off the public."

Fellow brothers and sisters of the 99% movement, I am here to share with you that leadership does not have to be a dirty word. Yes, it is rare, but there are godly leaders out there who are truly servants of the people, who put the needs of others before themselves. Leadership and management founded upon truth and goodness, comprised of men and women of virtue and pure motive can be a reality, and this type of new paradigm governance is the destiny of our planet. The Occupy movement has some soul searching to do and important decisions to make. I hope that in their consensus process they come to a consensus that a new system of leadership is needed and that good leaders are found and followed.

Occupation Of The Nation

by *Kazarian Giannangelo*

Much of the concepts within this article are inspired by the writings by Gabriel of Urantia.

Over the past few months, I have had the privilege of travelling the country with the Global Change Multi-Media street team to witness and film the Occupy movement first-hand and to present the Spiritualution[SM] movement.

We heard about Occupy Congress in early January 2012. Online it was billed as "the largest Occupy protest ever!" and encouraged citizens to gather outside of the Capitol Building on January 17 while the House of Representatives convened for the first session of 2012. Furthermore, the gathering encouraged occupiers and dissidents to make appointments with their state Representatives and engage them at the Capitol. Occupy Congress was a great idea. So great that my comrades and I knew that in mid-January, we would be travelling 2,000 miles to our nation's capital.

Congress was reconvening after the three-day, Martin Luther King, Jr. Day weekend. With Dr. King's legacy of activism, we imagined that there would be a substantial presence on MLK Day in Washington, D.C. We scoured the Internet for marches and demonstrations and quickly found Occupy the Dream, a gathering of "members from the African-American faith community [who] have joined forces with Occupy Wall Street to launch a new campaign for economic justice inspired by the legacy of Dr. Martin Luther King, Jr." In Washington, D.C. Occupy the Dream was holding a demonstration outside of the Federal Reserve, while at the same time similar marches were staged outside of fifteen other Federal Reserve buildings in cities across the country. Between Occupy the Dream, Occupy Congress, and an obligatory visit to Occupy D.C. at McPherson Square, we knew that we would have a full schedule.

Part 1: Occupy The Dream

You will have light in the night, shining so bright.
It's not by power or might, but by the spirit's light.

~ TaliasVan,
from his song "Listen To The Calling"

On that bitter cold Monday morning in January, we emerged from the D.C. Metro station, maps in hand, walking along Constitution Avenue looking for Occupy the Dream. I had watched the newsreel footage of Dr. King's famous "I Have a Dream" speech a few days earlier and expected to see an ocean of people covering the National Mall, standing shoulder to shoulder; hanging on the every word of a charismatic, black preacher. As we approached the demonstration I had to abandon my lofty expectations and occupy reality.

There were about a hundred people gathered on the sidewalk, all circled around a well-dressed man behind a microphone, while behind him was a cadre of activists and supporters standing in front of the Federal Reserve building. The man preaching was Dr. Jamal Bryant, pastor of Empowerment Temple, a 7,500 member church in Baltimore, Maryland. Bryant was one of the main organizers of the event and served as master of ceremonies. In his speech, he cited Dr. King saying, "Injustice anywhere is a threat to justice everywhere." Before introducing the other speakers, Bryant reminded the crowd that "This is not an event, this is a movement," and encouraged everyone present to follow the Occupy movement.

Bryant welcomed United States Marine Corps veteran Sergeant Shamar Thomas to address the crowd. Thomas is an Occupy Wall Street supporter from New York City who became an overnight celebrity when a YouTube video was posted of him, very vocally confronting NYPD officers in Times Square. Thomas is a force to be reckoned with. He has a he-man physique and the most gentle and gregarious spirit you will ever encounter. He too paid homage to King in his speech recognizing him as a man of faith who was willing to organize the people and motivate them to become activists.

After Thomas spoke, Bryant approached the mic to introduce Farajii Muhammed, a Muslim youth-leader from Baltimore. Muhammad spoke of the next generation and our responsibility to provide them with a world worth living in. After he spoke, he led the crowd in marching back and forth along the sidewalk, chanting in call and response style, "We fight to live, and not to die. We want justice, so we occupy." We marched for an hour or so before

Dr. Bryant gathered up the crowds for final statements followed by a closing prayer which he ended by saying, "The scripture reminds us, 'it's not by might, nor by power, but God.' We need your spirit. And in the words of our revolution, we declare, 'we shall overcome, today!' And those of you who believe it, instead of saying amen, shout Occupy!" And they did, and it was good.

Part 2: Occupy D.C.

There is a recipe for breaking popular movements... It goes like this. Physically eradicate the insurgents' logistical base of operations to disrupt communication and organization.

~ Chris Hedges, from his article "Occupy Draws Strength From The Powerless"

The sun was downing, but activity was picking up as we meandered our way through the streets of Washington into McPherson Square, the other "Freedom Plaza." We arrived in a spirit of reunion. Occupiers from across the country were arriving. Drummers were drumming and a pair of vivacious Occupy D.C. librarians were frantically trying to weatherproof their mobile research unit because Tuesday's weather forecast called for rain.

The first person I ran into was Jesse Lagreca, another Occupy Wall Street celebrity made famous by a viral video of him confronting FOX News. I had met Lagreca in New York during Occupy Wall Street's first months in Zuccotti Park and was glad to see that he had made the trip to be in Washington for Occupy Congress. Minutes after running into Lagreca I met an Occupier that I had been following on Twitter to receive Occupy Congress updates and another young man that I had met at Occupy San Diego. We met Occupiers from Portland, Seattle, Los Angeles, Oakland, Asheville, Boston, and New York. This was the gathering place of the movement, and it was happening all around us.

It reminded me very much of Occupy Wall Street. I was in Zuccotti Park for four days in October 2011 and witnessed a certain spirit of hope and revolution. In the half-dozen Occupy camps that I have visited since, Occupy D.C. came the closest to that spirit. It was by no means clean or well-organized, but there was a camaraderie that united everyone. Some folks had been camped out at Occupy D.C. for more than three months, since October 1, 2011. They had survived the systematic eviction, nationwide, of the majority of Occupations from their respective camps. We were able to witness that spirit of dejection first-hand when we visited Los Angeles the week after Occupy L.A. was evicted from their camp. But that chilly diaspora had not yet touched our nation's capital. (It was nearly a week after our visit that Metro Police forced the Occupiers to leave McPherson Square.)

It was getting dark and cold. We knew that the next day was going to be big, so we looked for the nearest train to take us toward our lodgings. We had been uplifted by McPherson Square, but across the street at the Metro station we were starkly reminded that not all of the 99% were at Occupy D.C. There in the dusky glow of the Metro station, was a small group of homeless people sitting against the wall trying to keep warm. Directly above them, in a wry and ironic display of inequality, was the official D.C. Metro sign offering directions to the White House.

Part 3: Occupy Congress

A demonstration should turn you on, not turn you off.

~ Phil Ochs,
American protest singer & songwriter

Several hundred people were gathered in front of the Capitol when we arrived, but no one knew what to do. One wild-eyed occupier in an orange jumpsuit mic-checked the crowd, trying to inspire everyone to storm the police barricade. "Why aren't we moving in more on our capitol? Here's our chance, right now, let's get f--king moving!" It was met with a listless response while another demonstrator responded, "The revolution cannot happen with five-hundred people."

Like Occupy D.C. the previous night, Occupy Congress was more of a gathering than a demonstration. People from all across the country had made it to the west lawn of the United States Capitol, a symbolic monument of democracy. Upon arriving, we immediately recognized people that we had met from other Occupations. It gave me a sense of how intimate the Occupy movement still is. There are not yet masses of people involved; it is a relative handful of dedicated individuals. The media likes to make a big deal out of Occupy as being a "leaderless movement." What Occupy really needs is more followers.

When I first heard about Occupy Congress, I signed up on an email list to keep up to date with developments. I was amazed at the amount of conflict that arose between the various organizers and others commenting from the sideline. Some wanted to pursue permits in order to have a legal demonstration, while others thought applying for permission to assemble was kowtowing to an unjust system. Some wanted to schedule a march while others wanted the event to be more "in the moment." Green Party presidential candidate Jill Stein tried to sign up for a spot on the open mic and all hell broke loose. Half of the people felt that it was not right to limit anyone from using an "open mic" and that it promoted communication. Others vehemently denounced the use of the event for political purposes. As one organizer wrote, "Politicians are a direct expression of the problems we are fighting against, it doesn't matter what kind of person they are or the platform they use. Politicians act against our interests simply through existing—they derive their power from our loss of autonomy. There should be no outlet for them to participate." Even before the event began there was division in the ranks, what few ranks there were.

The first thing we witnessed on January 17, 2012 was an official Occupy Wall Street spokesman approaching a very popular, well-known independent journalist and calling him a "snitch" on his Livestream/Internet broadcast. Weeks after the incident, these two Occupy brothers were still suspicious of each other and slandering each other online. One thing is for certain, these divisions will destroy the Occupy movement. It is imperative that Occupy develop an appropriate method of conflict resolution.

Meanwhile, throughout the day at Occupy Congress, there were some exciting moments. Someone did storm the police barricade and was arrested. After a General Assembly, most of the protesters left, en mass, to demonstrate on the steps of the Raeburn House Office Building. The Raeburn Building is across the street from the Capitol to the south. It houses about a third of the offices of the United States House of Representatives. As the daylight waned, hundreds marched to the Department of Justice and the White House.

Changing the world sure does work up an appetite, so we decided to Occupy a local establishment for dinner. We were seated in a quiet Thai restaurant when the highlight of our day walked in. A few blocks away, masses of angry protesters were gnashing their teeth in the dark when two unassuming men walked in. They sat at the table next to us looking like long lost brothers. One wore a suit and tie; the other wore a shirt that read "Occupy." We could not resist talking to this mismatched pair and asking them what brought them out to dinner together. It turns out they met in the gallery of the Capitol while they were both attending that day's session of congress. The guy in the tie was a congressional aid from South Carolina on his first day of work. The guy in the T-shirt was one of the congressman's constituents and an Occupier. We were close enough to hear to a lot of the conversation between this liberal Occupier and this young conservative politician. I am still not sure who picked up the tab, but I have no doubt that these two young men made deeper and more real, lasting impressions in each other's lives than all the mobs screaming at the police and cursing the Congress. This meaningful interaction would have never occurred without the all-call to Occupy Congress, but how different the day could have been if more individuals would have taken time to seek understanding, instead of being so demanding.

I'm convinced that if we are to get on the right side of the world revolution, we as a nation must undergo a radical revolution of values. We must rapidly begin the shift from a thing-oriented society to a person-oriented society.

~ Martin Luther King, Jr.

In the end, it is about people, not policy. Of the demonstrations I attended in Washington, D.C. in January 2012, I feel that Occupy the Dream was the most successful. It was not the most well-attended, but the people there listened to each other, respected one another, and supported each other during the entire demonstration. The individuals that attended Occupy the Dream walked away feeling more in love with their fellow man and woman. They prayed together and stayed together marching up and down a block of sidewalk. It contrast to the other gatherings of far-reaching tribes of rabble-rousers, Occupy the Dream was a tight-knit family; they stood united. The Occupy movement can take a lesson from the black church activists who have managed to focus their aim and in so doing, strengthen their power of change.

Submission And Transparency Versus Rebellion And Darkness. Inside Anarchy And The Black Bloc

by Amadon DellErba

Amadon DellErba is the son of
Gabriel of Urantia and Niánn Emerson Chase

Much of the concepts within this article are inspired by the writings by Gabriel of Urantia.

I am not an anarchist; I am a change agent. I have dedicated my life to the best of my ability to bring about change for the betterment of humankind. I live a purpose-driven life, and my daily actions are planned and calculated to inject change at some level—big or small, local or global. I try to live the philosophy: "Be the change you want to see in the world." This is the basis of my spiritual, moral, political, and material ideals. Change starts within, and I have discovered that at times it is hard to change myself.

I am a believer in "radical unity"[1]—when we step away from the labels, isms, dogma, doctrines, and ideologies of religions and political groups that divide humanity. We are no longer a Muslim or a Jew or a Christian; we are ascending sons and daughters of the Creator. We are no longer a Democrat or a Republican or a Libertarian or a Socialist; we are all one planetary family. This is radical unity. It is radical because it has never happened globally. It is a departure from tradition and is innovative and progressive. In order to adopt this mindset and live it, we must question every established doctrine and system known and created by humans and test their validity as being beneficial for humans and the environment.

Since autumn of 2011, I and my Global Change Multi-Media colleagues have traveled to several states to cover and participate in demonstrations within the 99% movement. We were given that opportunity because we strongly believe in the Spiritualution^{SM} movement—Justice to the People— which is a spiritual revolution movement that calls for a rising of consciousness globally. It is the expansion of our minds that allow us to grasp a broader understanding of the world and gives birth to the desire for justice to be manifested for all people of all nations and cultures. This broadened cognizance allows for more tolerance of and selfless service to our fellow humans. I believe this is how world change can happen—one person at a time, one unified group at a time, one movement at a time, one nation at a time.

Traveling the country, east coast to west coast, I shared the concept of a Spiritualution movement with many Occupiers and activists from all walks of life and experiences. I shared thoughts, philosophy, and concepts with many great and ambitious minds—minds that have risen out of the apathy that this country vaccinates its people with, which is meant to retard the beneficial but highly contagious bacteria of caring, of being aware, and of being willing to change. This beneficial bacteria is what the Spiritualution movement as well as the Occupy movement is. Corporate-owned media is the means of vaccinating people with narrow knowledge, complacency, apathy, and even ignorance.

I bore witness to the spread of an idea, from mind to mind across the country and world that started a spark in the oppressed and awakened the hearts of those who were sleeping. I am excited that people of all ages, races, religions, and backgrounds are taking part in the Occupy movement. I think that this could be the beginning of a global Spiritualution consciousness that needs to take place.

One group that I encountered was the Black Bloc that has been present at the demonstrations all across the country. I began to learn more about what separated me from the schools of thought they subscribe to. It is the intangible intellectual and spiritual beliefs that separate us. It is my ideology, principles, and faith that distinguish me from those who proclaim themselves anarchists, and it is understood by most other protestors and demonstrators that those of the Black Bloc are anarchists in their philosophy and strategies.

I do not believe in acts of violence or screaming insults at police who are just peacefully standing by and feel that such things are adolescent and non-effective. However, I do believe in taking a stand and putting your butt on the line for what you believe in, or in many cases, do not believe in, and this is where I found some commonality with some of the individuals of the Black Bloc.

In my encounters with a few individuals of the Black Bloc, I was afforded the opportunity to practice what I believe in—radical unity. How could

I work with and identify with those who challenged my beliefs and way of life? I learned much by realizing that at first I made mistakes in some of my assumptions and categorizing. But I also found common ground and was able to have good interaction with Black Bloc individuals in several states.

What Is An Anarchist?

There is no precise answer to the question of what an anarchist is. In fact, there are many different answers and ideas. What I found most interesting is that I asked a self-proclaimed anarchist in D.C. if he could describe what anarchy is. What he said was dramatically different than what the man I met in New York said, which was different from the guy in Los Angeles, which was different from the woman in Phoenix. They all had very different personal understandings of what anarchy is, as well as different ideas of adherence to the many and contradicting principals of anarchy, but they all labeled themselves anarchists.

I understand anarchism to be a political philosophy that holds any form of governance to be undesirable, unnecessary, and harmful. Thus anarchism opposes any type of authority or hierarchal organization in the conduct of human relations. Anarchists advocate a stateless society based on non-hierarchal voluntary associations. The term anarchism derives from the Greek word anarchos, meaning "without rulers."

There are many types and traditions of anarchism. Some of the schools of anarchism are: mutualism, individualist anarchism, social anarchism, collectivist, anarcho-communism, anarcho-syndicalism, and the list goes on. Anarchist schools of thought can differ fundamentally, supporting anything from extreme individualism to complete collectivism. And though these schools of thought have different ideals that can contradict each other, there is one unifying concept among them all, and that is to abolish authority. I often heard at the demonstrations anarchists scream, "F—k authority!"

Beyond the specific factions of anarchist thought is "philosophical anarchism," which embodies the theoretical stance that the state lacks moral legitimacy without accepting the imperative of revolution to eliminate it. In abandoning the hyphenated anarchisms (i.e. collectivist-, communist-, mutualist- and individualist-anarchism), it seeks to emphasize the anti-authoritarian view common to all anarchist schools of thought.[2]

As I participated in various Occupy events around the country, person to person and state to state I began to see among the anarchists the lack of unity and organization in the absence of a unifying consciousness and planned-out strategy. I began to see that the many Occupiers (and even some of the anarchists) did not want to be labeled "anarchists" by the media. The direct actions and diverse tactics used by the Black Bloc, which was the most prominent group of anarchists visible at these 99% protests, as well as other anarchists were often violent and non-effective acts of aggression towards police officers. This caused the general protester in the street to divorce himself or herself from that group.

I discovered that most Occupiers desire more commonality with the majority of citizens because they recognize that the 99% movement is about the issues of the majority. So, Occupiers want the majority of citizens to identify with them, at least on some issues they are protesting, and not be as exclusive as the Black Bloc and other anarchist groups are.

Protesting With The Black Bloc At The ALEC Convention

In November 2011, the American Legislative Exchange Council (ALEC) had its yearly convention in Scottsdale, Arizona. ALEC is a non-profit organization with members comprised of legislators and corporations. Corporations like Exxon, Wal-Mart, and Monsanto get together with governors, mayors, congressman, lobbyists, etc. and talk about how they can pass bills and change policies so that they can all make more money together. It is basically a cesspool of the power-elite's scheming about how they can gain more power and profit-making abilities through legislation, which too often oppresses and exploits 99% of the people in the almighty U.S.A., as well as in other countries.

My friends and I figured this would be a great place to meet new activists and talk about the Spiritualution movement. We also decided it would be a great time to live stream the protests online so that we could spread truth globally, educate people about ALEC, and advocate civil disobedience and fighting for justice.

Upon arriving we struck up a conversation with a street medic. As we conversed, he shared with me the code to text message so that I could receive the mass texts of alerts and updates from the protest organizers. I entered this into my phone not thinking much of it. (Later that day an address would be texted to me that directed us to a meeting place, but more on that later.)

This was my first time live streaming on the Internet. As I filmed what was happening before me, I excitedly narrated the arrests, pepper spraying, signs, and chanting of the crowd around me. The Black Bloc was at the frontline of the crowd of about 300 people and had flags and large black sheets with the red anarchist 'A' symbol on them. Seeing this, and assuming that they identified themselves as such, I narrated to about 400 people watching the live stream what the "anarchists" were doing. Things like, "the anarchists have stormed the police line and have created a non-peaceful situation while other protesters are chanting, 'Keep it peaceful.'" I reported on what I saw happening, delineating the anarchists from the rest of the protesters in my vernacular. I later learned this was a mistake.

About an hour into streaming, three of the Black Bloc protestors started walking briskly and aggressively towards me. Needless to say, I felt endangered and took a defensive stance. Two of them had masks on and one man did not. The maskless one shouted as he walked towards me, "HEY! Are you the a--hole who is live streaming? I just got a call from a friend who said you are talking shit about the anarchists." I responded, "I am the one live streaming." He then reached and grabbed my right arm and tried to yank the phone out of my hand. In defense, I responded by cupping my left hand and striking out at him, which disoriented him and he backed off. I made a few statements, making it clear that I would defend myself if he tried to physically attack me again.

I tried very hard to diffuse the conflict with words rather than fists, and it worked. We had a ten-minute argument about my rights to live stream. They did not want their faces filmed and did not want to be publicly labeled "anarchists" but as the "Black Bloc." I agreed to no longer refer to them as anarchists and let them know that I had not been filming their faces and did not intend to. I also let them know that I had been unaware of their not wishing to be called anarchists, even though that is what they were. This type of agreement was enough for them to back away . . . for the time being.

Six hours and eighteen arrests later, the protest ended. Soon after, I received a text message from an anonymous sender about meeting at a particular address to discuss the next day's actions. I figured this was from the main organizers and was excited to meet them and talk about our actions for day two of the three-day ALEC convention. My friends and I got in our car and entered the address into our GPS and the calm voice of "Robo Girl" led us there.

As we walked up to the location, there was a group of about eight people in a circle talking outside. I smiled and said, "Hey guys." They all stared at us coldly and bewilderedly, saying nothing. I then noticed that they were all dressed in black. I think I even recognized some of the eyes and foreheads from the morning's protestors since the rest of their faces had been covered early that morning! I thought, "That is cool, some of the Black Bloc came to meet too." My friends and I kept walking this narrow alley between two buildings, and when we turned the corner, our eyes grew large, our hearts started beating a little faster, and our adrenaline kicked in. Before us were about fifty people of the Black Bloc in this hidden junk-yard area—all dressed in black and all eyes on us. Until then, we had not known that this was the gathering place (of twenty-two years) for the radical underground of the Phoenix Black Bloc.

Instead of turning around and fleeing the place, we walked right on in. There have not been many situations in my life where I felt that I would have to physically defend myself, but this was one of them. My nerves were tight, and so were those of my three friends. We started scanning the perimeter for all exit routes and potential weapons we could use to protect ourselves against any attack. I have never been in a situation where I felt so much animosity from a collective group. My friends looked to me for the signal to leave. In spite of all of this, I pulled up a chair and sat down, even though I was very uncomfortable sitting, which was not the chair!

The physical environment was chaotic and dark, with minimal lighting. All around us was junk that had been arranged into some semblance of art. There was a fifteen-foot-high tower of stacked shopping carts with a couch on top and the anarchist flag flying high. I felt like a squirrel surrounded by coyotes, all eyes glaring at me, and my friends felt just as vulnerable.

I sat there and systematically scanned the whole crowd, looking at anybody who looked me right in the eyes. I then saw my assailant from early that morning and looked at him and nodded, not sure what I was communicating with my body language other than, "I am here, and I am not afraid. Let's talk."

We were not attacked, and during the twenty minutes before the actual meeting began, my friends and I had a few conversations with some people from Occupy Phoenix who had happened to drop by for the meeting. Mostly I just observed and listened to the conversations around me. Finally a woman announced that the meeting would commence. About fifteen of the main people who represented their various working groups gathered in the inner circle for the meeting, with everybody else gathering around it. All decisions were concluded on consensus. A woman introduced the various things they needed to cover in the meeting. The first priority was a "security concern" that needed to be addressed. All agreed on the agenda of the meeting, and it started with a young woman who stood up from the inner circle, pointed her finger directly at us and said, "We want to know who you are and why are you here." I then proceeded to briefly explain who my comrades and I were and why we were there. After minimal conversation between us, she offered that they take a vote if people wanted us to stay or not. Within five minutes they went around the circle and each person shared that we should leave, that there was nobody to vouch for us, and that we were likely undercover cops. We were asked to leave with a very intense energy, making it clear that we would be escorted out in any manner necessary if we did not comply.

On my way out the man who attacked me that morning came up to me and apologized in his own way. I did the same and spoke to him for a few minutes but had to hurry out as people started shouting, "Leave!" and "Get out!" I patted him on the shoulder and made peace with him and left. But the next day at the protest, he was at it again in a verbal attack on me with two others because they thought we were not who we said we were but were undercover FBI agents, which my friends and I thought was paranoid on their part.

Radical I Am

What divorces me from the general mindset of anarchy is my embrace of hierarchy and my submission to authority. This submission is not to any past or modern system created by man to further greedy control and exploitation over others. My submission is the recognition of those people in my life that I would consider spiritual elders and guides, counselors, teachers, and leaders who assist me to be a change agent in service to bettering our world. It is adolescent, and ultimately destructive, to reject all forms of leaders and organizational structure.

Because I grew up in a community that was founded on leadership—a board of directors and elders—and a definite hierarchical structure, I was afforded the rare and distinct privilege of witnessing true and balanced leadership. I was able to experience what so few on the planet have—guidance and direction from leaders who actually care about your well-being and the common good of all.

Because the good leaders in history, as well as currently, have often been overshadowed by the terrible and at times extremely inhumane leaders of the past and present, many people have a very skewed and limited perspective of a society based and built upon leadership. Many people have little point of reference or examples of what a truly just leader is, but this is not the case with me. And it is not the case with more than one hundred other people who have been a part of one of the largest and longest-sustaining EcoVillages in this country. I grew up in this new paradigm and alternative culture. I prescribe to no doctrine of man and state. I believe in a society with proper leaders and authority because I know what a true administration is—of and for the people.

It is foolish to think that social evolution can take place without visionary leadership, strategic foresight, and decisive actions. It is the submission to a higher reality of co-operation and community living that will conquer the unjust oppression of the power elite. It is the fearless rejection of mediocrity and conformity to a sick society that will challenge the injustice of this world. It is the transparency of truth and righteousness that will crystalize change.

I do not just rebel against the corrupt parts of a system, because doing so is recognizing that the system has the power over you. No, I completely divorce myself from that corruptness. I completely reject parts of the system that have fallen to selfishness and greed. I am part of creating a new system, a system of cooperation and unity, radical unity. My consciousness is my radical action.

There is nothing radical about violence and destruction. How is that a departure from the norm? How is throwing rocks at police and breaking windows radical in the sense that it is new and innovative? It is not. People have been throwing rocks and destroying for thousands of years. It is time to create, to build, and to forgive so that the forgiven can begin anew in a new system.

I live a purpose-driven life. My purpose is to be a part of bringing change to this planet and to confront injustice before me and in me. It is in the acceptance that I must change myself to be a better change agent, that I can appreciate the elders in my life who help me do that. This is the only authority I come under. This is radical. It is radical to be a 21-year-old man and to come to someone who has gone long before you and say, "I need help in this situation. What can I do here?" It is radical to place my trust in another who I deem worthy and be willing to do what is asked of me and directed.

Perhaps some would argue that I am not strong enough to lead myself and that I am mentally weak and need others to make decisions for me. No, it is just the opposite. It is that I am whole enough and mature enough to know that there are other people who have more wisdom and knowledge than I do, that there are many people I can learn from. Many youth today never grow out of the mindset of "F—k authority." Into their thirties and beyond they engage in adolescent actions, often thinking that they have to be burned by the fire themselves in order to realize it is hot and dangerous because they do not trust anyone telling them that it is and thus preventing their own pain. In general, I think that American society teaches kids that they need to burn themselves in every metaphorical fire of life to understand that it is hot, that you cannot just trust somebody else to let you know that it is hot, and therefore not do it. This is foolish and detrimental to the maturation and growth of the mind, body, and soul.

We cannot build a new world without the consciousness of love and submission to goodness and beauty. I reject the darkness of fear, distrust, and destruction. I wear no mask, and I do not consider myself a coward. I stand before you and proclaim what I believe in under no veil of fear. My heart beats in rhythm with my mind, making me a more unified and whole being.

I have been Occupying my entire life. I have been Occupying a lifestyle where equality, opportunity, and justice prevail over greed and power. I have been Occupying an intellectual and spiritual mindset that grants me true liberty and opportunity that our Founding Fathers wanted for the citizens of this country. I am Occupying ideals that lift me from the muck and mire of slavery to tradition and false dreams of opulence and selfishness. I am Occupying the pursuit of truth that is always evolving, creating, and demanding change. I am Occupying the fight for justice that gives me esteem and confidence to reach out and help another. I am Occupying my heart's ideals without compromise, which grants me transparency to wear no mask, for I am proud of who I am and what I stand for.

    I am Occupying Avalon Organic Gardens & EcoVillage. I live in an adobe hut built in 1921, surrounded by a herd of goats, gardens with rows of vegetables, and a windmill of fresh well water. This is my freedom from the 1%.

Photo Gallery

Including photos of each Occupy city where the Global Change Multi-Media and Global Change Television team traveled to cover the stories and support the movement.

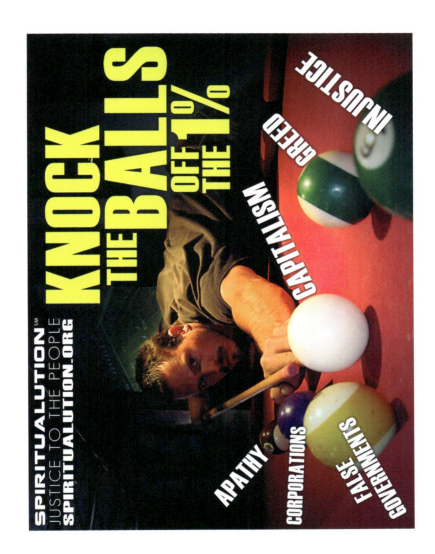

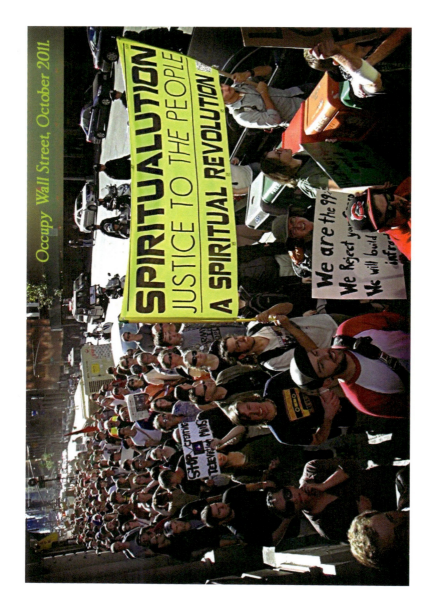

Occupy Wall Street, October 2011.

Amadon DellErba interviews actress and activist Susan Sarandon at Occupy Wall Street, October 2011. To view the complete interview, go to Spiritualution.org

Gabriel of Urantia speaking at Occupy Tucson, October, 2011.

Global Change Music nonprofit record label band Van'sGuard performing at Occupy Tucson, October 2011.

Occupy Tucson March on the Banks, November 2011.

Protesters calling to shut down ALEC (American Legislative Exchange Council) in Scottsdale, Arizona. November 2011.

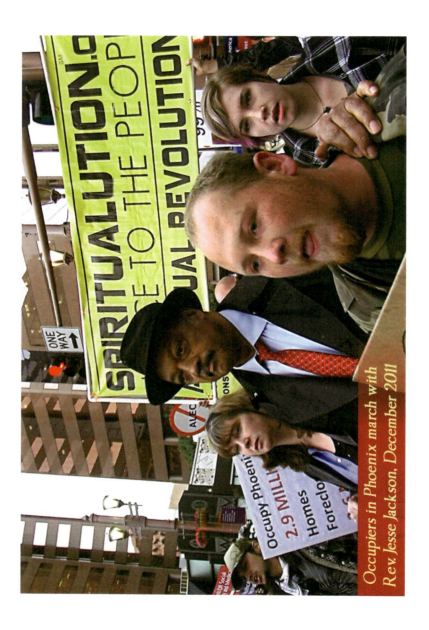

Occupiers in Phoenix march with Rev. Jesse Jackson, December 2011

A day of action to shut down the ports.
Long Beach, California · December 2011

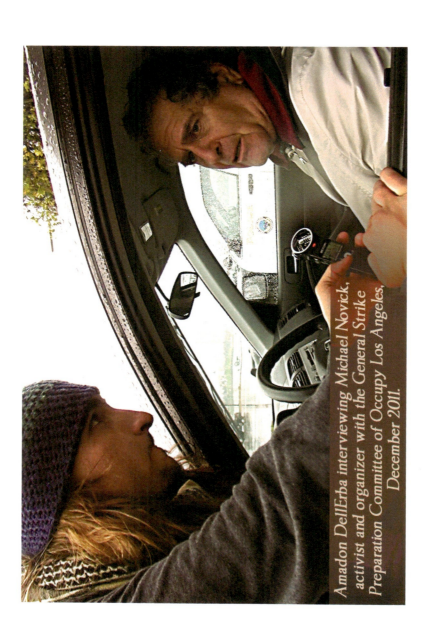

Amadon DellErba interviewing Michael Novick, activist and organizer with the General Strike Preparation Committee of Occupy Los Angeles, December 2011.

The Spiritualution street team joins Occupy protestors in Green Valley, Arizona, a retirement community south of Tucson. December, 2011.

Bringing the Spiritualution message to the U.S. Congress, January 2012.

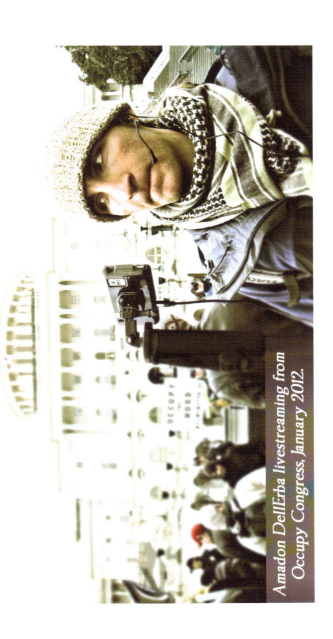

Amadon DellErba livestreaming from Occupy Congress, January 2012.

TaliSeen and DeleVan of Van'sGuard at Occupy Congress, January 2012

Sergeant Shamar Thomas, USMC veteran, interviewed by Amadon DellErba at Occupy the Dream in Washington, D.C. January 2012.

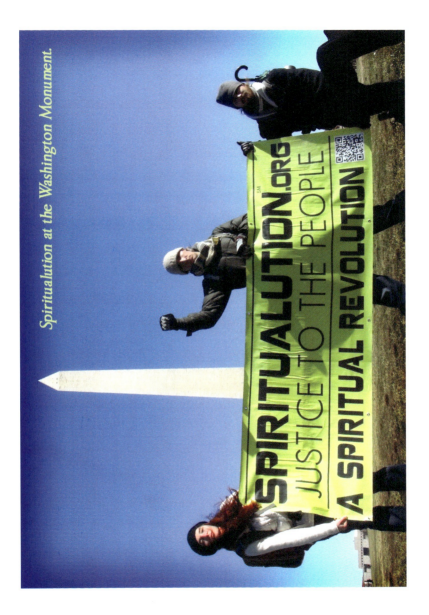

Spiritualution at the Washington Monument.

Spiritualution sign shown on Russian Television report of anti-NATO Protests in Chicago, May 2012.

Patch Adams being interviewed by Amadon DellErba at the anti-NATO protests in Chicago, May 2012. Amadon is the son of Gabriel of Urantia and Niánn Emerson Chase. To view the complete interview, go to Spiritualution.org

Anti-NATO protests in Chicago, May 2012.

Rev. Jesse Jackson speaks with Amadon DellErba at the anti-NATO protests in Chicago, May 2012.

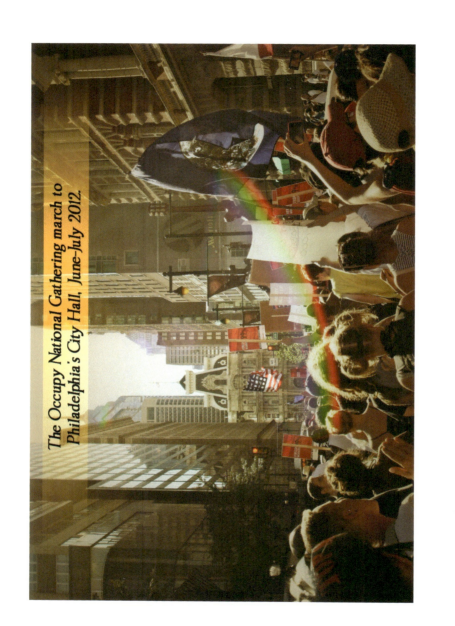
The Occupy National Gathering march to Philadelphia's City Hall, June–July 2012.

Amadon DellErba interviewing Truthdig.com columnist Chris Hedges at the Occupy National Gathering in Philadelphia, June–July, 2012.

The Spiritualution team hits the streets of Philadelphia, June–July 2012.

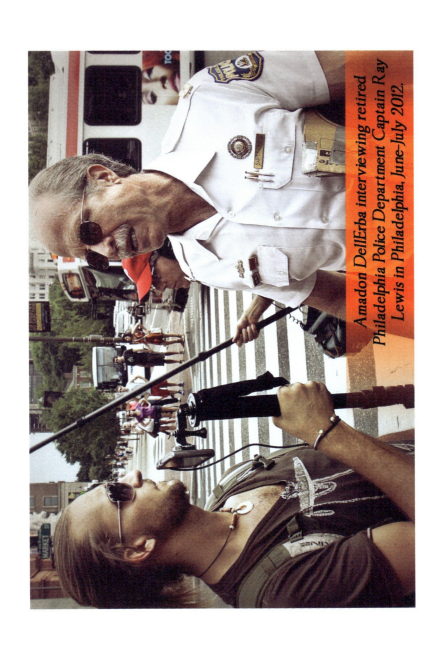

Amadon DellErba interviewing retired Philadelphia Police Department Captain Ray Lewis in Philadelphia, June-July 2012.

Protests against police brutality and violence in Anaheim, California. July 2012.

Amadon DellErba interviewing Sonia Hernandez at the protests against police brutality and violence in Anaheim, California (July 2012). Her brother Martin was killed in March 2012 by Anaheim police.

Anaheim, California.
July 2012

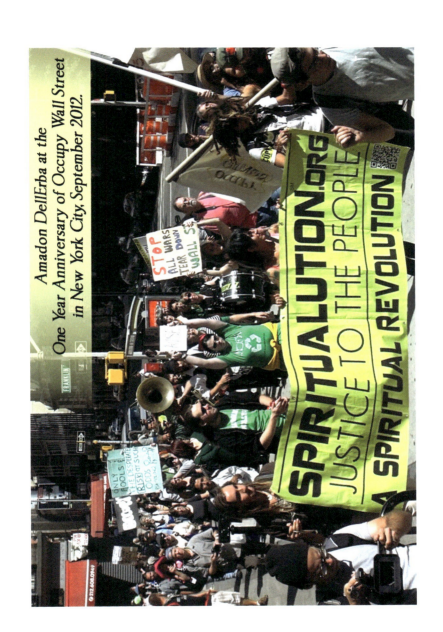
Amadon DellErba at the One Year Anniversary of Occupy Wall Street in New York City, September 2012.

Amadon DellErba at the Anti-Spectra Oil Pipeline Environmentalist March in New York City, September 2012.

Anti-Spectra Oil Pipeline Environmentalist March in New York City, September 2012.

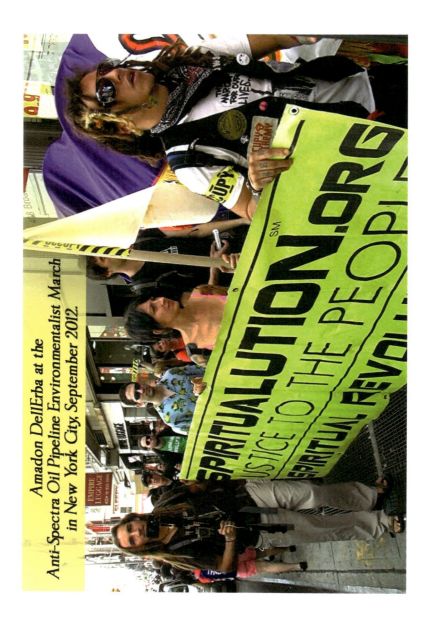

Amadon DellErba at the Anti-Spectra Oil Pipeline Environmentalist March in New York City, September 2012.

Amadon DellErba at the One-Year Anniversary of Occupy Wall Street in New York City, September 2012.

Amadon DellErba being arrested by NYPD at the 1-year Anniversary of Occupy Wall Street, September 17, 2012

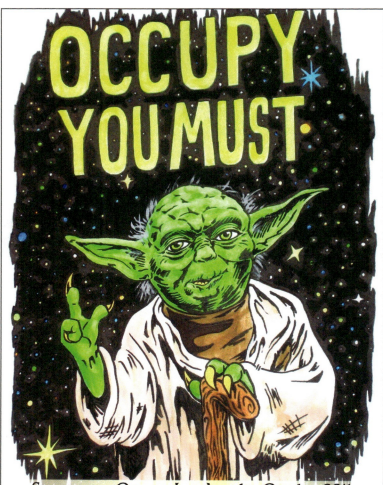

Street art at Occupy Los Angeles, October 2011.
Photo by R of the Northeast L.A. Radical Neighbors
(http://la.indymedia.org/news/2011/10/249221.php)

A Hands-in-the-Soil morning at Avalon Organic Gardens & EcoVillage.

Cal-Earth dome homes at Avalon Organic Gardens & EcoVillage.

Construction of a Cal-Earth dome home at Avalon Organic Gardens & EcoVillage.

Solar Panels provide shade to our automotive workshop.

Caring for young broccoli transplants at Avalon Organic Gardens & EcoVillage.

Papercrete bricks such as these are used in building projects throughout Avalon Organic Gardens & Eco Village.

A 5,000 gallon water tank is used to store harvested rainwater outside our solarium and bath house. Solar panels on top the building heat water for the bath house.

Transplanting lettuce at Avalon Organic Gardens & EcoVillage.

Global Change Music nonprofit record label band VansGuard at the Earth Harmony Festival, October 2012 • vansguard.org

Amadon DellErba, drummer for Van'sGuard

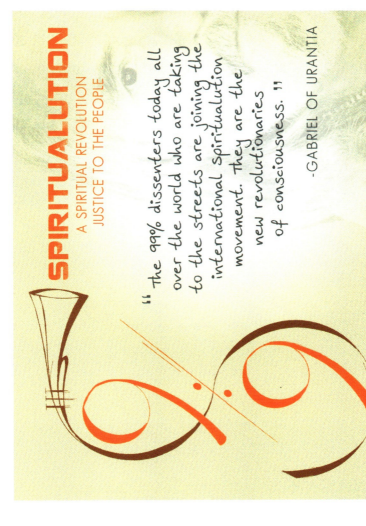

THE SPIRITUALUTION^{SM} MOVEMENT

SPIRITUALUTION — JUSTICE TO THE PEOPLE

A global spiritual-revolution, designed to inspire and influence millions to come out of the system of greed and organized and antiquated religions, and join communities, and grow their own food near a good water source, as Gabriel of Urantia believes in the prophecies of the Hopis, Mayans, Nostradamus, the Prophets of the Old Testament, and the Book of Revelation that speak of the purification of the Earth Mother through drastic climate changes, which he believes are now happening and will continue to worsen.

THE SPIRITUALUTION MOVEMENT IS:

- Active dissension against injustices and creating opposition in action
- Action against corporate corruption, not just hoping and praying for change
- Developing standards of morality in viewing Hollywood films and independent films and not allowing these films to destroy our minds and the minds of our children and grandchildren, by not buying these films or going to these movies
- Resisting evil in all its forms

- Being kinetic not apathetic, not just observing evil or overlooking it but energetically acting against it. Creating a synergy of resistance
- Civil disobedience instead of private complaining
- Not letting any entity impinge upon your freedoms
- Boycotting all chain stores owned by mega-corporations and products sold by them and buying locally in your neighborhood and supporting your local economy
- Not just buying organic food (free from toxic chemicals sprayed by corporations), but growing your own gardens and becoming sustainable and self-sufficient without depending upon energy and poisoned sustenance from corporate powers

These Spiritualution points, and more, are just the beginning steps of true spirituality. It is not joining an organized religion or church and falling into the doctrines of man, but listening to the voice of the Creator, as He guides you out of the third-dimensional entrapments and into the fourth-dimensional reality of light and life to come.

The need for unity among believers in the Creator on this confused world is of utmost importance. Throughout the epochs of history, the Creator has given epochal revelation to bring humankind together under the one Creator.

There have been five epochal revelations on the planet in the last 500,000 years—the Fifth being *The URANTIA Book* and the continuation of it, found in *The Cosmic Family* volumes.

All believers in the Creator as a personality must put away the doctrines of man that separate humanity and come together in the love of the Creator, which is what true religion is all about.

Humanity must begin to expand its consciousness of the vastness of the Creator and the Creator's creation. It is essential now that a Spiritualution movement take place and we come together in radical unity against religious dogma, fundamentalism, and narrow-mindedness.

One God, One Planetary Family
~ Gabriel of Urantia

spiritualution.org

Below is a recent law passed by the Congress and signed into law by President Obama that you should know about.

National Defense Authorization Act (NDAA)

"On December 31, 2011, President Obama signed the National Defense Authorization Act (NDAA), codifying indefinite military detention without charge or trial into law for the first time in American history. The NDAA's dangerous detention provisions would authorize the president — and all future presidents — to order the military to pick up and indefinitely imprison people captured anywhere in the world, far from any battlefield."

source: http://www.aclu.org/blog/tag/ndaa

Following are some important issues on gun control.

House of Representatives bill in motion in the 112th Congress

H.R. 367:
Freedom to Serve Without Fear Act of 2011
112th Congress, 2011–2012

To prohibit the knowing possession of a firearm near a venue at which a Member of Congress is performing an official and representational duty or campaigning for public office.

source: http://www.govtrack.us/congress/bills/112 hr367

From Gun Owners of America
posted Tuesday, 05 April 2011 18:25
on gunowners.org

H.R. 367
(Richardson): "This bill would make it a ten-year felony to 'knowingly' carry a firearm within 250 feet of a building where you 'know' a member of Congress is. Thus, the bill would create an incomprehensible series of moving 'no-gun' zones. And while, for example, you would be exempted for a gun in your house, if you lived next door to a congressman, you could not carry your gun to your car parked on the street."

source: http://gunowners.org/hr367.htm

Comments on gun control by Gabriel of Urantia

The 1% definitely would want arms taken out of the hands of Americans. So would all enemies of America. What keeps America safe from invasion is the fact that every other American has a weapon and can defend themselves, not only from murderers and thieves but from invading armies. Every citizen becomes a citizen soldier then.

I do believe that many automatic pistols, rifles, and assault weapons should not be sold to citizens, and there needs to be better screening and documentation of who buys any weapon, and when any public servant speaks to the general public, they should automatically be given police protection freely.

Global Change Music[SM]

Global Change Music lyrics speak of a Spiritualution[SM]—Justice to the People concept of a spiritual revolution (where spirituality means social action, not pious, hypocritical religiosity). The lyrics speak of taking action against any form of those injustices where the people are oppressed. Global Change Music promotes sustainable living, which includes growing your own organic food, building green, permaculture, sharing services and goods (trade and barter), and having a protective environmental consciousness. The music itself can be any genre, however, the musicians must live their message of national and international radical changes.

BE AWARE PROCLAMATION

Be Aware of ... Popular False Leaders and Attacks on True Leaders

- Of the common people's need for true spiritual and political leaders (which should be basically one and the same).

- Of the misrepresentation and demonization of true spiritual or political leaders, poets, and activists by status quo newspapers, television, radio, and other media.

- Of the realization of who the false leaders are, including false executives, ministers of state, journalists, and others who do not use their Creator-given talents for the betterment of humankind.

Be Aware of ... Greed

- Of the unethical corporate entities ripping you off, taking your money, and keeping you in slave labor, making them rich.

- Of the control of the masses by the rich, who own and operate the production, supply, and distribution of food and water.

- Of the unequal distribution of wealth, supplies, and material goods, keeping the poor fighting among themselves.

- Of college students taking out loans that, in today's economy, cannot be paid back to their debtors, thereby enslaving these students for life.

- Of the inability of the poor and disenfranchised to get grants or scholarships to try to better their lives through education.

Be Aware of ... What You Buy

- Of the need for more green products and for people to live more sustainably, decreasing consumerism and materialism.

- Of the need for people to demand cheaper prices for solar power equipment and other energy-saving practices.

Be Aware of ... What You Eat

- Of the poisoning of our food, water, and air.

- Of the chemicals and toxins in most of the foods, that are actually non-foods manufactured by greedy, non-caring companies.

- Of the need to buy locally and to grow organic gardens wherever people can.

Be Aware of ...   The Medical Industry

• Of the lack of proper health care and high costs of medical services. We need free universal healthcare that will truly serve the poor and disenfranchised with quality comprehensive care, not more empty promises from legislators.

• Of the media brainwashing you to make you think you've got some kind of disease, so you can buy more drugs and products.

Be Aware of ...   The Hollywood Delusion

• Of the need to stop attending movies and music concerts that are made solely for sex, violence, and greed and have no positive message for humanity.

• Of the idolization of movie stars, rock stars, and sports heroes who receive way too much money as compared to teachers and public servants.

Be Aware of ...   The Failing Infrastructure

• Of the failing bridges and dams that can collapse any day, killing hundreds and thousands of people who live near these dams and cross these bridges. Example: 13 people were killed and 145 injured when a Minneapolis, Minnesota bridge over the Mississippi collapsed in August 2007.

- Of the failing electrical power plants. Example: The 3-day, August 2003 blackout, affecting 10 million Canadians and 45 million Americans in eight states.

- Of the misappropriation of American taxes; trillions of dollars being spent on war instead of repairing our failing infrastructure.

Be Aware of ... Chemtrails

- They are dropping aluminum particles from the sky, destroying natural crops and seeds so that geo-engineering can take place worldwide. Therefore the only food we will be able to grow and eat are genetically-modified foods. This aluminum from the chemtrails is also causing many health problems including autism, Alzheimer's, and lung and heart problems.

    The main proponents of this are Monsanto and the power-elite, who want to make every farmer and citizen dependent upon buying genetically-modified foods and also may be insane enough to actually want to decrease the population by these toxins and poisons. Where these perpetrators live there are no chemtrails.

- Solution: Write letters to your congressmen and Senators, who may not be aware this is even going on. You would be surprised of how many are uninformed and think the chemtrails are just exhaust jet streams from airplanes.

There is an excellent video out on this called, *What In The World Are They Spraying?* It is produced by Michael Murphy, an independent journalist and political activist from the Los Angeles area whose work focuses on issues that go beyond the interest of the mainstream media. It is free online to see the full-length documentary.

Be Aware of ... The Times

• Of the increasing distortion and delusion energies on the earth, leading to multiple/mass killings, airplane and train crashes, and acts of hate and terrorism (see *The Cosmic Family, Volume I*, Paper 215).

• Of the increased separation of the good seed from the bad seed, and the obvious behavior of good people becoming better and evil people becoming more iniquitous.

• Of the positive signs of the return of the Promised One to set up His Divine Government. Examples: Signs in the sky, UFO sightings, crop circles, and 1111 being seen on clocks and other digital devices—a sign of the return of the Promised One from the 1111 loyal Midwayers.

The "Promised One" is also known as the Hadhrat Isa (the Arab name for Jesus—Islam), Kalki Avatar (Hindu), Jesus Christ (Christian), Maitreya (The World Teacher—Hindu/Buddhist sects), Jampa (Tibetan), The Messiah (Jewish), Krishna (Hindu), and Imam Mahdi (Muslim). The Promised One is also known by many names in indigenous cultures.

NOTE: The Promised One is not on the planet at this time, and all reports of this are false. When The Promised One returns everyone will know about it.

• Of the days of purification, tribulation, and the possible destruction of the earth through the fulfillment of the prophecies of the Mayans, the Hopi, Nostradamus, the Prophets of the Old Testament, and the Book of Revelation. Examples: severe weather changes, earthquakes, tornadoes, tsunamis, volcanoes, plate-shifts, plagues, asteroids, and/or nuclear war.

• Of the adjudication of the Bright and Morning Star versus Lucifer and the end of the Lucifer Rebellion and the beginning of the first stage of light and life (see *The Cosmic Family, Volume I*, Paper A).

Answers To The Be Aware Proclamation

1. First, come to the Creator and make the Creator your personal Guide and Friend. Seek the Creator's perfect will and listen to what you are told. You will be led to the correct spiritual teacher or teachers. You may be told to stop doing a number of things that are harmful to yourself and others. You may be told to leave the career or job that is not beneficial to all humankind and even to leave the present location you are in and go elsewhere to start a new career in the service of humankind where your talents can be better used to serve humanity. You must learn to trust in the Creator for your needs and not the fallen system. Seek friendships with others who have made this commitment to the Creator. Let the Creator guide you.

2. Get off of all drugs—cocaine, marijuana, the abuse of alcohol. Medical marijuana should only be administered with the aid of a spiritual advisor/shaman, of which there are few at this time.

3. Wisely choose the DVDs you watch, the movies you see in the theater, the books and magazines you read. Do not support needless violence (shoot 'em up, blow 'em up, crash-boom-bang!) and unnecessary sexuality that is not done in good taste, representing a historic and real-life story plot behind it. Write letters to producers to make films of more moral content, with messages that touch the human heart and fill the soul with emotions of love and hope.

4. If you are single, trust that the Creator has planned for you a future complement who is perfect for you so that you can be more at peace and do the things that the Creator would want you to do with your time, instead of going to places to look to find that complement in all the wrong places.

5. If you can, in time, start or join a community that grows their own food, is trying to get or is off the grid, has a water supply, and have all things in common. The near future will be more troubled with economic chaos, weather changes, and natural disasters.

UNOCCUPY YOUR COUCH
10 Points To Become Proactive In

1. Call friends and family about having a meeting to discuss ways in which you can participate in the Occupy movement.

2. Stop buying the products from the corporations. Consume less. Learn to live more simply.

3. Stop attending certain Hollywood films that have no positive message, except silliness, violence, and sex.

4. If where you are presently working is a bank (as a teller or above that position) quit your job. You are not serving the people. You are serving the 1%. Put your money in a credit union. Trust the Creator to guide you to a better job to serve humanity.

5. If you are working for a nuclear plant, an oil company, or an insurance company quit your job.

6. Talk to your friends and family about moving to the country and buying land near a good water source and growing your own food. Times ahead will be troubled and the Safeways (or other supermarkets) will not have the food your family needs to survive.

7. Stop going to sports events and paying high ticket prices so that the 1% owners become richer and the players become richer while our teachers hardly can survive.

8. Stop going to rock concerts and supporting degenerate rock stars. Do not give your children the money to do this.

9. The corporate news (ABC, NBC, CBS, Fox, and CNN) feed you propaganda every day. Watch instead Free Speech TV (on satellite 348) and Link TV (375). These stations are nonprofit and give you the more comprehensive news and the truth.

10. Instead of taking two-week vacations or more, volunteer your time off from work in humanitarian programs and spend the vacation money on necessary and emergency relief programs like: funds for rebuilding in Haiti and other devastated cities, the disenfranchised poor programs in America, food for Children International, Doctors Without Borders, the American Civil Liberties Union (ACLU), and the Southern Poverty Law Center. There are many other charitable organizations that could use your help.

5 PRINCIPLES OF PLANETARY PEACE

1. The rich would give most of their money away (that they really do not need) to the needy. They would become true philanthropists. The line between the rich and the poor would vanish.

- A responsible way to do this would be to give increments of money to respected and proven spiritual and church leaders so that they could disburse responsibly to the needy. This is the method Jesus used with the Apostles. The people gave to the Apostles, who in turn disbursed the funds to the people.

2. Free healthcare would be given to all, from babies to hospice. Any group of men who call themselves a government and who follow the First Commandment could not be in a government without this service to humanity.

- As long as the money system exists, all doctors should be given a livable salary and no more. Doctors first and foremost are healers, and this should be the reason for their calling, not profit.

3. Free education would be given to all students who wish it, no matter what the age.

- A national board of educators should be set up to disburse good teachers to various universities everywhere, so that education is equal in every university, as well as learning tools to be appropriately dispersed. This should extend to all levels and grades, from elementary to university.

4. Jobs would become careers, and all people would be placed in positions suitable to their experience, talents, and Creator-given destinies.

- A national board should be organized—who understand the differences between old souls and new souls—that can determine early talents and place people (souls) according to their unique abilities and astral experiences. EXAMPLE: New souls usually find themselves in physical construction, whereas older souls are the architects and designers. For more information read *The Cosmic Family, Volume I*. Please contact Global Community Communications Alliance for additional literature on the subject.

5. The Creator would not become a subject that people would avoid but a subject that everyone would talk about with each other, because The Creator is the Father of All. This would cause the end of all antiquated religions into one world, true religion—the religion of the Fatherhood of the Creator and the brother-/sisterhood of all humankind.

- The Fifth Epochal Revelation *(The URANTIA Book)* and Continuing Fifth Epochal Revelation *(The Cosmic Family* volumes*)* should be read, taught, and understood by all races and nationalities.

These five points are just the beginning. More advanced additional principles cannot come until the first five principles are practiced, because those more advanced principles would not even be close to being understood. But the first five, applied immediately, might save the world (and basically the lives of millions and millions of people) from its own self-destruction, through continuing earth changes and possibly world war.

Song Lyrics
by Van'sGuard

TO BE FREE

VERSE 1
Watched them cross the line time after time
Paid a time for the price of their lives
They're told to fight, it's trite, but still they fight
   with all their might
Chased dreams
Occupy the streets
Nothing is as it seems when you're trusting only
   in the unseen

CHORUS
They were crying there in the dark
He then told them, "Do you see that spark?"
Then they rose up wanting to be free
And he led them, carried them 'cross the sea

VERSE 2
To be free we need to really see
We're bound by the chains of fame's key
They say pay me now and we'll show you how
Then they steal your dreams . . . from under
   your feet
But that's OK 'cause you have wings
Set yourself FREE!

REPEAT CHORUS
They were crying there in the dark
He then told them, "Do you see that spark?"
Then they rose up wanting to be free
And he led them, carried them 'cross the sea

CHANT
We are the 99%
Justice to the people

Lyrics and melody available for ringtone at
spiritualution.org

Video available at
vansguard.org/media

For more information visit
vansguard.org

© 2011 Global Community Communications Alliance
All rights administered by Global Change Multi-Media,
P.O. Box 1613, Tubac, AZ 85646.
All Rights Reserved.

Notes

The Occupiers Must Learn How To Use The Creator To Win Over The Power-Elite And Their Soldiers Of Gas-Destruction

[1] Matthew 6:24 (KJV)

Submission And Transparency Versus Rebellion And Darkness. Inside Anarchy And The Black Bloc

[1] The concept of radical unity that I am referring to in this article was coined by Gabriel of Urantia

[2] *The Blackwell Dictionary of Modern Social Thought*, Outhwaite, William & Tourain, Alain. 2nd ed., p. 12

ABOUT THE AUTHOR
Gabriel of Urantia

Gabriel of Urantia is a cultural visionary, spiritual leader, social and political change agent, environmentalist, musician, father, activist, and author.

His wisdom and fidelity to teaching truth has placed him into a distinct position as a leader among people who hunger for change. His activism is not tokenism; he lives and breathes it. His past and present actions are a clear indication of his lifelong struggle to bring about positive and lasting global change.

In 1996 he developed his "Spiritualution^{SM}—Justice to the People!" concept, a spiritual revolution for and by the citizens of Earth. It is not the raising of arms but the raising of consciousness and each individual's own commitment and willingness to change—to quit their wrong jobs and to go on strike. It has inspired and influenced thousands to take action against social, civil, and environmental injustices and to be proactive in their spirituality.

Because Gabriel of Urantia's work has rocked the status quo in many realms of influence, he has come against much opposition and media misrepresentation from corporate powers and the power-elite. His insistence on spiritual revolution and spiritual unity has not made him popular amongst established religious groups. His teachings on unity without uniformity have challenged the dogmatic and antiquated religious minds of the masses. Gabriel of Urantia has shown that he will not cease in his efforts to bring a higher truth to the world through what he has called "Radical Unity." He calls out to humanity to come together under the banner of equality and justice.

For decades now, visionary pioneer Gabriel of Urantia has been telling the American public and the world—through his books, videos, music concerts, and publications—that they must take to the streets through civil disobedience against the power-elite and corporate entities, which include corporate media, the banking system, the oil companies, the corruption in the government, and more.

He specifically emphasizes, for those who cannot participate on the streets in civil disobedience, that many millions of Americans can and should participate by going on strike and quit their jobs, if their jobs or careers are not serving humanity, such as:

— Bank employees (which even includes tellers). If the banks have no workers they cannot operate or stay open. As long as capital exists in this world, we have to open "People Banks"—owned and operated of the people, by the people, and for the people.

— Nuclear plants and weapons factories

— Genetic seed engineering facilities that destroy our organic and native seeds

Let your conscience be your guide on other jobs and careers you should leave.

The 99% movement and the Occupy Wall Street movement are the beginning stages of Gabriel of Urantia's teachings to the people of America taking place in physical manifestation.

Global Community Communications Alliance and Divine Administration

Global Community Communications Alliance is a church supporting: a religious order and EcoVillage of 100+ international members living in community (with thousands of local and international supporters); Avalon Organic Gardens & EcoVillage; Personality Integration Rehabilitation Program for Teens and Adults; Global Family Legal Services. In addition Global Community Communications Alliance's affiliates and supporting nonprofit organizations—Soulistic Medical Institute and Soulistic Hospice, and Global Change Multi-Media—also support ministry programs.

Founded in 1989 by Gabriel of Urantia (gabrielofurantia.info, gabrielofurantia.net, gabrielofurantia.com, gabrielofurantia.org) and Niánn Emerson Chase (niannemersonchase.org), Global Community Communications Alliance is located in southern Arizona in the charming, historic southwest towns of Tubac and Tumacácori—a sacred area known as "the Palm of God's Hand."

Find out more about our many local and global related humanitarian efforts, services, and church programs listed:

Worldwide Sunday Services^{SM}
Open to the public.
(520) 603-9932

Avalon Organic Gardens^{SM} & EcoVillage
165-acre farm and ranch in southern Arizona, using spiritually-based principles and permaculture practices. Community Supported Agriculture (CSA) provider.
avalongardens.org • (520) 603-9932

Soulistic Medical Institute^{SM} & Soulistic Hospice
Offers healthcare by professionals whose expertise involves various healing modalities that encompass the soul, mind, and body.
soulisticmedicalinstitute.org
(520) 398-3970
soulistichospice.org • (520) 398-2333

Personality Integration Rehabilitation Program^{SM} for Teens and Adults
Assisting socially-disappointed souls in their psychospiritual healing process.
pirp.info • (520) 603-9932

Friendly Hands Vocational Training^{SM}
Spiritual Training Apprenticeship Programs in a wide range of career fields.
(520) 603-9932

Global Family Legal Services℠
Legal aid in various fields focusing on immigration
for low-income individuals and families in need.
globalfamilylegalservices.org
(520) 398-3388 or (928) 282-2590

Spirit Steps Tours℠
Offering enlightening tours for the seeking
sojourner and eco-tourist.
spiritsteps.org
Toll-free (866) 508-0094 or (520) 398-2655

Global Community Communications Schools of Ascension Science & The Physics of Rebellion℠
Teachings from the Continuing Fifth
Epochal Revelation, *The URANTIA Book*
and *The Cosmic Family* volumes.
gccschools.org • (520) 603-9932

Global Community Communications Schools for Teens and Children℠
The only school on the planet for teens and children
incorporating the soul's point of universe origin
and soul age, enabling the child to be guided into
their correct destiny at a much younger age,
bringing much earlier actualization, fulfillment,
and self-confidence to the child.
gccschools.org • (520) 603-9932

Out of the Way Galleria℠
An eclectic blend of created art contributed
by local artisans and donors.
outofthewaygalleria.org • (520) 398-9409

Planetary Family Services^{SM}
Provides services to create, embellish, and bring Godly energy to your home environment.
planetaryfamilyservices.org
(520) 403-4207

Global Change Multi-Media^{SM}
globalchangemultimedia.org
(520) 398-2542

Divisions of Global Change Multi-Media:

Future Studios^{SM}
Recording studio.
futurestudios.org • (520) 398-2542

Global Change Music^{SM}
Nonprofit record label offers musicians recording opportunities using professional world-class equipment for voice and instrumental training.
globalchangemusic.org
(520) 398-2542

The Musicians That Need To Be Heard Network^{SM}
Provides opportunities for musicians to communicate their music messages without spiritual compromise.
musiciansnet.org • (520) 398-2542

Global Change Radio[SM]
Internet radio station offering on-demand audio webcasts, including talk radio on various religious and social themes.
globalchangeradio.org • (520) 398-2542

Global Change Television[SM]
Internet television station with a variety of programs of spiritual content, on demand.
globalchangetelevision.org
(520) 398-2542

Music & Films at The Main Stage, Tubac and The Sea Of Glass, Tucson
Working with filmmakers and distributors of independent, activist, and educational films and documentaries that motivate spiritually thought-provoking group dialogue for the public. Booking national and international bands.
(520) 398-2542

Global Change Theater Company[SM]
Dedicated to writing, performing, and staging plays and various higher-consciousness, inspirational, dramatic productions where students receive training and opportunities to participate in theatrical shows and workshops.
(520) 398-2542

Global Change Multi-Media Distribution Company℠

Distributes music, DVDs, books, magazines, and any product that would be considered by its parent company to be a Global Change Tool for the dissemination of revelation and spiritually-uplifting information through media materials.

Global Change Multi-Media Productions℠

Professional audio, video, and Internet service producing spiritual and educational message media, via Internet video streaming, live webcasting, graphic design, and CD and video/DVD media production.
(520) 398-2542

Global Community Communications Publishing™

Publishing continuing epochal revelation and related materials as well as Global Change Teachings and other spiritually-oriented texts.
gccpublishing.org • (520) 603-9932

Alternative Voice™

Quarterly periodical that addresses the many crises of our world, fusing spirituality with activism.
alternativevoice.org • (520) 603-9932

The Sea Of Glass — Center For The Arts
Venue – Music – Art – Dance – Multi Media –
Theater – Healing Arts
Nonprofit organization
330 E. 7th Street, Tucson (4th Avenue area)
TheSeaOfGlass.org

Food For Ascension Café
Organic Raw Food & Juices & Teas
330 E. 7th Street, Tucson (4th Avenue area)
FoodForAscension.org

Sacred Treasures
Clothing (men's & women's), arts & crafts
330 E. 7th Street, Tucson (4th Avenue area)
Sacred-Treasures.org

CosmoArt Studio
See artists' works-in-progress & art
330 E. 7th Street, Tucson (4th Avenue area)
CosmoArt.org

Global Community Communications Alliance

P.O. Box 4910, Tubac, AZ 85646 USA
(520) 603-9932

e-mail: info@gccalliance.org
gccalliance.org
globalchangetools.org

Seminars, Workshops, & Internships

Sustainability Seminars, Internships, & Workshops:

Green Building, Permaculture, Using Greenhouses To Extend The Growing Season, & Organic Gardening

- On survival in the near future, organic gardening, and the nuts and bolts of building an EcoVillage.

Held at Avalon Organic Gardens & EcoVillage
in Tumacácori, Arizona
or
Held in your city

Contact (520) 603-9932
email: info@avalongardens.org
http://avalongardens.org

http://avalongardens.org/sustainability-seminars

Divine Administration Seminars (for serious spiritual seekers)

- Working together in conjunction within the Divine Mind.
- Ascension Science and the Physics of Rebellion.
- Could you be a Destiny Reservist?
- What is an Audio Fusion Material Complement and the Mandate of the Bright and Morning Star?

Held at Avalon Organic Gardens & EcoVillage in Tumacácori, Arizona

Contact (520) 603-9932
email: info@gccalliance.org
http://gccalliance.org

http://gccalliance.org/divine-administration-seminars

TO ORDER
globalchangetools.org
or TOLL-FREE 866-282-2205

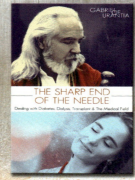

The Divine New Order
Gabriel of Urantia's
Autobiography
paperback $16.00

The Sharp End of the Needle
Dealing with Diabetes, Dialysis,
Transplant & The Medical Field
paperback $25.95 / hardback $31.95

The Cosmic Family, Volumes I and II
Ascension Science & The Physics of Rebellion
Volume I - 393 pages
paperback $29.95
hardback $39.95

Volume II - 567 pages
paperback $34.95
hardback $49.95

TO ORDER
globalchangetools.org
or TOLL-FREE 866-282-2205

Teachings on Healing
135 pages
paperback $14.95
hardback $19.95

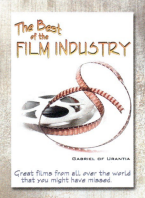

The Best of the Film Industry
more than 1,254 film reviews
paperback $13.95

The Real Santa Claus
(in English y en Español)
hardback $19.95

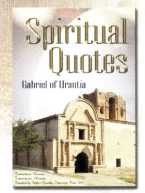

Spiritual Quotes
paperback $9.00

TO ORDER
globalchangetools.org
or TOLL-FREE 866-282-2205

CosmoPop® Music
Lyrical and Melodic Masterpieces

TALIASVAN
& The Bright & Morning Star Band

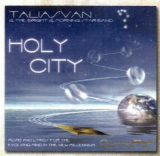

Holy City
CosmoRock, CosmoFolk,
& CosmoCountry
$16.00

CosmoPop Millennium
$16.00

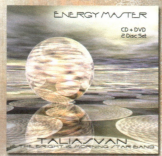

Energy Master
CosmoMystic
CD and DVD set
$21.00

CosmoPop Variety
CosmoRock, CosmoFolk,
CosmoMystic, & CosmoCountry
$16.00

Gabriel of Urantia is also known as TaliasVan
& The Bright & Morning Star Band with his music career.

TO ORDER
globalchangetools.org
or TOLL-FREE 866-282-2205

CosmoPop® Music
Lyrical and Melodic Masterpieces

TALIASVAN
& The Bright & Morning Star Band

3-song introduction to
CosmoCountry
$10.00

The God Child Came
Christmas Album
$14.00

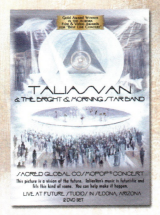

Sacred Global CosmoPop
Concert DVD 2-disc set
Live from Future Studios
in Sedona $21.00

The God Child Came
Christmas Play & Album
CD / DVD set $21.00

TO ORDER
globalchangetools.org
or Toll-Free 866-282-2205

TALIASVAN'S
40-VOICE BRIGHT & MORNING STAR CHOIR & ORCHESTRA

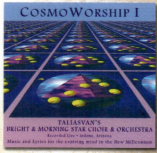

CosmoWorship I
$14.00

CosmoWorship II
$14.00

other GLOBAL CHANGE MUSIC bands

Van'sGuard
Live at Avalon Gardens
Earth Harmony Festival
3 songs $9.00

Starseed Acoustic
Ensemble
Interuniversal Home
$13.00

Other titles by Gabriel of Urantia available from
Global Community Communications Publishing
A Division of Global Change Multi-Media

*The Divine New Order And
The Dawn Of The First Stage Of Light And Life*
by Gabriel of Urantia
Autobiography of Gabriel of Urantia and
the history of the beginning of
Global Community Communications Alliance.

The Cosmic Family, Volume I
as transmitted through Gabriel of Urantia
Continuing Fifth Epochal Revelation,
Papers 197–228 succeeding *The URANTIA Book.*

The Cosmic Family, Volume II
as transmitted through Gabriel of Urantia
Continuing Fifth Epochal Revelation,
Papers 229–261 succeeding *The Cosmic Family, Volume I.*

Messages To Urantia, 1997–2000
as transmitted through Gabriel of Urantia
A collection of 19 sacred messages from celestial beings
addressing the state of our world, Urantia.

Teachings On Healing, From A Spiritual Perspective
by Gabriel of Urantia and Niánn Emerson Chase
Teachings focused on bringing about healing
on the physical, mental, emotional, and spiritual levels.

*The Best Of The Film Industry
—Movies You Don't Want To Miss!*
compiled by Gabriel of Urantia
A detailed list of commentaries and reviews of films
that educate, challenge, and expand the consciousness.

***Making The Most Of Media Exposure For Global Change
Versus Our Experience With The Media***
by Gabriel of Urantia and Niánn Emerson Chase
Firsthand account of experiences with
corporate-controlled media.

Spiritual Quotes
by Gabriel of Urantia
A collection of spiritual insights and wisdom
addressing many of life's facets.

The Real Santa Claus
by Gabriel of Urantia
A children's book sharing a unique perspective on who really
is the beloved Santa/St. Nicholas of Christmas.

The Sharp End Of The Needle
by Gabriel of Urantia
A compelling story of personal experience with
diabetes, dialysis, kidney transplant, and
the positive and negative aspects of the medical field.

CPSIA information can be obtained
at www.ICGtesting.com
Printed in the USA
LVIW010759241112
308634LV00001B